UNBIDDEN GARDEN

A SOUTHSIDE HOOKER NOVEL — BOOK 3

BAER CHARLTON

MORDANT MEDIA ™ ®
A Division of Charlton Productions

Nina Golemi, Cover Creative Art
Rogena Mitchell-Jones, Editor, www.rogenamitchell.com
Mar Penner Griswold, Content Editor
Laura Reynolds, Illustrator

ISBN-13: 978-0-9849666-3-9 (paperback)
Published by Mordant Media, Portland, Oregon
10 9 8 7 6 5 4 3 — 2019 Edition

MORDANT MEDIA ™©®
A Division of Charlton Productions

ALSO BY BAER CHARLTON

Death in the Valley – Book One
Light to Light – Book Two

BOX

CHAPTER ONE

THE DRIVER SWORE in the rain. Everything had gone wrong. The heist, the car, the road, and that didn't include the weather soaking the driver's clothes wet and cold.

The driver tugged on the leg, drawing the body out through the shattered window, and then taking up the second leg like a small burro with a cart. The largest of the bodies, thankfully, was tall but thin. The body bounced and tumbled along the streambed rubble. Only a slight relief came from the swelling of the small December stream. It would become larger with the winter rains. The body floated for a moment and then caught on the rocks of the other side. The driver kept dragging.

The light mist had turned the dirt road to a snotty slide now wept the blood of the driver into larger patches about the clothes the driver wore. The blood from the other man's head curled and danced down the stream, washing away into the late night, screeds of something becoming, and then disappearing.

The driver breathed hard, dragging the body up the small incline to the shallow flood-washed cliff-side cave. Pulling the taller man by the clothes and body parts, the driver fed the warm corpse into the natural tomb. The driver stopped for a moment and looked at the expensive diving watch on the body's wrist.

Quietly, the left hand smoothed over the short hair from the body's forehead. The driver sat thinking of the last few years. Better times.

In the distance, a flash of lightning cracked, and the boom of thunder rolled across the South Bay Area and up into the low coastal mountain range. It wasn't supposed to be like this.

The driver twisted and continued pushing the body into the cramped, shallow cave next to the other smaller body. Finally, the feet were needed to push and roll the larger body up and on top of the smaller to make room for what was still to come. The driver reached in and closed the now opened eye, hand hovering for a moment, and then withdrawing.

Slogging back down the damp incline, the driver once more crossed the small stream, and with dispatch, noted the volume had increased. The hills above would have been getting rain for more hours before. It was now flowing downhill.

The driver kicked at the back door of the car. With a long slender limb, the driver pried the complaining door partially open. Wedging their body into the gap, the driver began to work on widening the access. The screaming of the steel was loud. The driver wasn't worried. The nearest house was probably well over two miles away. And even if it were next door, the sound of the rain and storm would have just made it another noise during a dream in the night.

"Shit."

The last body was pounded into a ball and pummeled down into the leg area between the driver's seat and the back seat. With the car mostly upside down, it was obvious a great force had placed him there. Only the left arm hung free into the space of the car.

After stumbling among the large rocks and flood bed wastage and stubble, the driver clawed around the back of the car, pulling through to the front window. The car had spun-out above, rolled, and then flipped, causing the driver to be ejected on the second roll before the next flip had taken the car over the hundred-foot slope to the stream bed below. The driver marveled at the durability of the car. As 1937 was a great year for Chevrolet, it had also been a terrible year for Chevrolet. The cars were almost indestructible. Now, nearly seventeen years later, they were still running.

The last pitched flip had thrown the car into the ravine eighty feet below and forty feet across the stream bed for one last roll.

The driver stooped and slid upside down through the driver's window. Arching and stretching while feeling for the seat release, it was obvious nothing seemed right upside down. The mutilation on the arm didn't help.

The large black Bakelite knob felt right. The driver tugged without a result. The lever didn't move.

"Shit."

The driver hung from the knob, thinking how the car had rolled over and righted, right hand becoming the left before orientation finally became solid.

The driver's hand jerked, and then jerked harder. The lever moved. A click and the seat jumped forward an inch.

The large body thumped sickly down onto the ceiling.

The driver hung for a moment from the knob. A slight, wan smile crossed the pale, freckled face; the right, lower lip, and the left upper sucked into the teeth at the same time. The driver was still thinking.

Scooting with back down face up, the driver started moving the last body toward the other side. Pushing feet against the window post and moving the body using upper body strength—shoulders, hips, legs, shoulders—each part pushed one at a time.

Exhaustion was taking a toll.

The eyes of the driver flashed open at the sound of a rock as it rolled down the hill and splashed into the deepening water. The cold was setting in, and it hadn't helped drifting off on a nap. The driver wearily eyed the small stream. It was rapidly becoming a much larger stream now moving rapidly.

The driver rolled over, realizing sleep had come with the driver's head in the face of the last body—the face of the one person who in life had been the most repulsive.

"Shit."

Moving with renewed vigor, the driver pushed the body

around until the legs were sticking out of the window. The body was now aligned to cross the now larger body of water. "You better float, you big tub of lard." Thinking, the driver realized the body's coat was insulated and still dry. The driver stripped the body of the warm, dry shirt and jacket.

Crawling out the other window, taking up the two feet, pulling and drawing the body out and onto the water—now waist-deep, the driver was relieved as the body floated.

"Now, if you could just float up the fucking hill, you asshole."

The swearing somehow lent a certain amount of indignant strength. The body fit almost perfectly in the hole, leaving a space for the last objects.

Crawling back into the car, the driver flipped the two custom latches. The back seat swung down, and the four large bags fell from their hiding space. "Shit." The driver, picking up one of the bags and realized it would take three trips. Opening one of the bags, they looked in, and then drawing one of the objects out—the driver whistled low.

As the sun began to glow through the clouds, a lone figure plodded along the road. The driver's fingers were torn up from digging the dirt to fill in the gravesite. This caused the driver to reminisce of times making fun of all the 4-H kids in school and how dirty their hands were—which was almost as horrid as how bad they always smelled—like wet animals. The farm kids were not much better.

No, sir, the driver had never wanted any part of raising animals or growing things and had damn sure never intended to plant a garden—especially not one as unbidden as the one just planted.

The driver washed off in the now hard-moving cold river. Not even hot water and soap would be able to remove the stain of the night's planting.

The driver turned up the collar of the oversized wool P-coat. It was a very long walk to Salinas down the low coastal mountain range. With any luck, walking the road known as *The Snake* would only take a couple of days.

CHAPTER TWO

THE SEMI-COLD AUTUMN rain captured in the dark curls irritated the large scars underneath. The drizzles continued down under the leather collar to the starched white T-shirt underneath. Hooker jerked harder on the towing cable jammed under the Cadillac. Hooker and the car were in a few inches of water where the car slid its way off the dirt road and down an embankment into the creek eighty-feet below.

In disgust, Hooker yelled up the cliff to the Squirt above. "Send me down the second cable." He looked down at how the Cadillac lay on its top. "Hey, Squirt?"

His head and shoulders appeared over the top of the cliff holding the other J-hook and cable from the second boom on the tow truck. "Yeah, boss?"

Hooker smiled. He really liked how this kid was getting smart and sassy. "Clip a girdle line and two ring cinches onto the cable. I'll have to drag this bitch up on her back and flip her up there."

"10-4, Bawana. Coming right down."

Hooker shook his head. The two months in the hospital had the kid watching every single old Tarzan movie they ever made. Hooker remembered whatever the kid sees or reads, he remembers forever.

Reeling out the cable, he hooked two iron J-hooks to parts of the undercarriage he could reach. Running the ring cinches through the eyes of the hooks, he attached the girdle line. Drawing it to the end of the main cable, he attached the girdle chains to the hook on the end of the cable.

"Okay, Squirt. Slowly roll the secondary."

"Taking up slack." The cable tightened and began to pull.

Hooker could sense the tension of a snag. The grinding sound through the cable stopped. Hooker smiled. The kid was starting to sense things through his fingers on the controls and by listening to the sounds of the cable or car.

Hooker knelt down and peered through the gloom at the crap helping to bind the draw hook to the undercarriage. Fishing his hand in the cold mud and gunk, he withdrew a large bone. Examining the muddy artifact haphazardly, he sized it up as he pitched it back across the river wash toward an old rusted heap. It hadn't had the benefit of being towed. Hooker mumbled, "Somebody doesn't have a leg to stand on." Fishing around some more, he unhooked the cable and hook while watching the approaching dark uniformed figure in rain gear. As he started to rise, he noticed a quick shine in the mud. Reaching down, he picked up an oval of some kind of heavy metal. He wiped most of the mud off and stuck the oval in the front pocket of his overalls.

Hooker looked up the hill to the head and shoulders looking down. "She should come now, Squirt."

The car scraped at the mud wall but moved just fine. Hooker turned to face the officer. The officer looked at the underside of the upside-down car. "What do you think?"

Hooker wiped his hands on the large shop towel from the back pocket of his overalls. "Well, Micha, I've gotta be honest with ya. I'm pretty sure the Fly can pull the engine and transmission back out of the front seat and fix the fire-wall, but the upholstery is shot." Hooker's right eyebrow was cocked at an up and back angle, something the long, new scar in his scalp was doing.

"No, I meant..." The California Highway Patrol Officer and friend for over ten years stopped and gave the smirking Hooker a hard glare. "I meant, how much longer until I can clear the road?"

Feigning innocence, "Oh, give me about forty or so minutes to drag this prom queen up to the road, and maybe another ten to flip her onto a dolly, five to hook her to Mae, and she's all yours." Hooker walked back to the working deck controls and started letting the car down onto the sling. "Actually, I don't have to dolly this one. The lady left her driveline down in the creek." Seeing the raised eyebrow of the officer, he reassured him of cleaning up the wreck. "Don't worry. I threw it in the back seat with a few other pieces of metal and bones."

They climbed up out of the ravine, and both were filthy.

Re-rigging the sling for towing, Hooker set the J-hooks around the axles and cinched the chains onto the small hooks of the sling. Raising the end of the heavy car, Hooker checked around the Cadillac and tested the sling. Shutting the control compartment door and scanning the working deck, he wiped his hands one last time on the rag and pitched it into the can for dirty laundry to be done as needed. Turning back to the officer standing several yards away, he jammed his lower lip over his teeth and whistled, wheeling his right hand and index finger in a circle. "Clear, Micha."

"Thanks, Hooker. We'll see you tomorrow for dinner at Dolly's place."

Hooker waved as he shucked out of his jumpsuit overalls. Nodding to the kid, he turned and climbed up into the high yellow cab of his restored 1959 Marmon truck. The low rumble of the idling engine charged the heater blowing all winter long across the floor and the cardboard box. The box was filled with twenty pounds of yellow and scarred tabby with only one ear and one eye. Drawing in his left leg, Hooker closed the door painted with the truck's namesake: Mae West, in all her World War II pin-up glory. A small banner ram down along her body emblazoned with the slogan 'It's what's up front that counts.' This was a reference to the largest production conventional truck ever built. Its recently customized front nose contained a sixteen-hundred-horse-powered engine. Mae West was the fastest tow truck in the five Bay Area counties. Even the little two-ton Fords with their new, hot 440 engines couldn't hold a candle.

Hooker looked over at the Squirt, who was smiling with a silly smirk. Hooker nodded his head up. "What?"

Squirt laughed. "We're on the Snake." He nodded at

the back end of Micha's retreating patrol car. "Even Micha knows we have to pass Thrifty's on the way to dump the prom queen, and he doesn't even eat ice cream—much less French vanilla."

At the sound of his favorite treat, Box stood up in his box. His one ear stuck up into the draped hand and fingers. The fingers began to pull and rub at the last vestige of his ear. The purr was instant and non-stoppable.

Hooker rolled his eyes. "Ganging up on me. Jeez, mareez in the deep freeze."

Forty minutes later, with both windows rolled down, the giant truck rolled past the time and temperature sign on the bank reading twenty-eight degrees. In the night air, leather elbows stuck out of each window, triple-scoop French vanilla ice cream cones in each hand. The sounds of Tex Ritter drifted sorrowfully into the night air.

CHAPTER THREE

"Just because it's only six-ten in the morning, don't you two even *think* about sneaking in without a kiss or hello." The disembodied voice of the consummate mother hen floated from the large sunroom around the corner.

Hooker raised his right eye at his companion as the Squirt slowly closed the giant hand-hewn walnut front door to Hacienda Romero. Hooker nodded his head forward for Squirt to follow.

"Lucy, we're home." Hooker imitated Ricky Ricardo on the *I Love Lucy* show, which none of them had ever seen because it would require a television.

Stella looked over her cheater glasses and the top of the newspaper. Her mouth pursed as she examined the two men standing safely still on the slate of the dining area and inches away from her cream carpet. She slowly lowered the newspaper. "Squirt, kindly take Hooker out into the front yard and hose him down. There is mud all over his boots and lower pant legs." She raised the newspaper.

As they turned to head for their bedrooms, Hooker leveled his right eye at the younger man. "You so much as point a hose at me, and I will make sure it takes a very good proctologist to find the back end of said hose." The two smiled as they separated for some much-needed sleep.

Five tows and the long hard recovery job had taken its toll on the two still recovering men. They each had two dimes floating around in them, which were delivered by a shotgun at the hands of a killer.

Box, unaffected by the work, but always ready for some rest, searched out his patch on the queen-sized bed and settled in. Hooker was only moments behind as his pants slid down around the uppers of his boots, fireman style. His head almost bounced once on the pillow before the phone in the main room rang.

Anytime the phone rang before nine or ten in the morning was never a good sign. Hooker's mind half waited and then was gone. Moments later, Stella stood outside the cracked door. The soft snoring told her the piece of paper in her hand could wait. She padded back to her morning domain of sunshine, laying the note on the large granite island as she passed.

Three in the afternoon would be soon enough for the man on the phone. It was just about some wrecked car Hooker had towed during the night. She was sure it wasn't anything important. After all, the kid needed his sleep.

. . .

HEAVY FIESTA WARE crockery makes a very distinct, dull bell sound when placed onto thick granite. When the thick plates finally land on a thick, hand-hewn black walnut table, the sound changes to the wet thud of two fat skaters colliding on ice. In Hooker's dream, it was slow cars sliding on black ice in the fog. The thought or vision of so many cars to be towed forced Hooker to spring into action mentally. The first requirement was to wake up and smell the coffee, which meant the golden payday wreck evaporated.

Hooker groaned as his legs begrudgingly swung over the edge of the bed. His right hand smoothed along his upper thigh and the deep trough of a long surgical scar—made to find and remove three dimes. The doctor counted the surgery as seventy-five percent successful. Rising, he padded his way toward the bathroom and a quick shower. As he sat on the toilet, he could hear Squirt already in the shower in the next bedroom suite over.

Box stuck his head in the bathroom and came over to rub along Hooker's leg. The hand found the cat's one ear and rubbed it for a good morning. Hooker reached his left hand over and around the cat's head. The fingertips found the chin and gave a firm rub. "Go tell Stella I'm up and will be in for breakfast in ten minutes."

Hooker wasn't positive whether the cat truly under-stood him or not, but as the cat left, Hooker did know he would go check in with Manny, who would then tell Stella 'in about ten minutes.' Of course, routine had nothing to do with it.

Hooker was still blurry-eyed as he opened his bedroom

door to find the other blurry-eyed zombie dressed identically in the uniform of the day—an obligatory starched white t-shirt over jeans. The other zombie mumbled something as they lined up to shuffle into the dining area.

Manny looked up and smiled. Stella turned at the stove and opened both arms wide. The two young men socketed in for their morning hug and rebounded toward the mugs of coffee standing by the percolator. Stella smiled at her two zombies. "Go sit, and I'll bring your breakfast."

With each bite or sip, the walking dead became human.

Stella slid the note into the purview of the half-alive Hooker. She was greeted with a bloodshot eyeball over the rim of the mug.

"He wanted to know if there were any other body parts he should know about." She nodded her head forward and gave Hooker the same deadeye of a zombie. Only Hooker knew where or when it had started, much less why, but the zombie look had become a family joke for dumb questions begging for dumb answers. It had all come down to shorthand for how one felt the morning after, or don't ask because Manny has been on the phone all day. Even Manny occasionally rolled his head back with a gaped mouth to comment on something as innocent as being asked what he wanted for Sunday dinner—the answer always being pot roast.

Hooker looked at the note. Allen was the 'back door' man at the Fly's auto body shop. Every wreck towed in went through Allen's hands, fell under his eye and was sorted with the same discernment he had shown as a corpsman in Vietnam—before an exploding shell had taken his right leg, leaving bits and pieces of metal in the man's body. His favorite joke about the metal floating around in his body was he had more in common with the cars than any other swinging dick in the joint. He never mentioned the large steel plate covering most of the right side of his head. The ridges were very distinct on his abnormally bald head. In fact, he had no hair left on his body anywhere. For that, his nickname was 'Dog' as in hairless Chihuahua.

Hooker laid the note down and picked up his fork in his right hand. The Squirt absentmindedly withdrew his left hand out of striking distance. The four snickered. The four tiny dot scars were still evident on the back of his hand from the night he had met Hooker. Hooker's fork had been buried in Squirt's entire hand except for the last few layers of skin on the palm. Hooker didn't know then the street tough who was trying to steal a dollar from the tip on the counter was the waitress's little brother. Candy, the waitress and the girl Hooker wanted to date, sorted everything out. Hooker and Squirt's friendship had seen rapid growth over the next week to the point where the Squirt had taken twenty-four dimes in his body and legs as he saved Hooker's life.

Manny, ever the consummate detective, nodded at the cryptic note. "Really... a skeleton hand found in the car, and you're not just a little bit curious?" The man leaned back in his custom wheelchair. Hooker continued to ignore him and kept eating.

Manny looked over at the silent Squirt, who seemed very busy examining his scrambled eggs and pancakes. He was working very hard to try to ignore Manny, as well. "Is there something wrong with your eggs, Squirt? Because, if there is, you need to speak up so either I can fire the chef or have her give you a lap dance."

The young man turned a very dark shade of red and almost choked as he focused harder on his food. Stella put her fork down and gave Manny a hard look. Picking up her coffee mug, she stood and strode to the counter to fetch the coffee percolator. Pouring some in her own mug, she stood staring out the window at the large barbecue deck, thinking.

She turned with the unplugged coffee percolator and walked over to stand next to Hooker. She stood looking down at the top of his head of wavy dark hair, parted with two large scars running the side of his head. This was where twin dimes had seared their way along his skull, slicing open the covering of both skin and hair, as they had passed at nine-hundred feet per second. "Hooker, you have two choices here. You can talk to your father, and drink this coffee, or you can start wearing all one hundred and eighty degrees."

Hooker's head snapped up and looked at Manny. "There was a leg bone at the wreck site, also. I thought about going back out today sometime and poking around with the Squirt to see what else might be there." He hadn't wanted to tell Manny and Stella because he knew the retired detective's badge was—in the words of his wife—still attached. Hooker was also hyper-aware that the last two mysteries had taken their toll on the whole family. The hot brown liquid of life at Hacienda Romero flowed unimpeded into the large mug.

There was no way in hell Manny was going to even

smirk, much less smile, and lose this contest. With every bit of his decades of control in the face of adversity, or playing the deadpan face-off game, Manny asked the next question. "Right or left?"

Coffee and bits of pancake shot from the Squirt's nose. He looked up to see by the faces of the other three he had just lost the round. With the loser established, the others laughed as Stella stepped over to the large granite island and got the poor loser a towel.

Hooker wasn't about to let Manny get the upper hand, though. "It was dark, but I think it was the right tibia. I remember thinking any other remains would be all that was left."

A tiny bit of coffee missed the Squirt's rapid swallow. He mopped at it with the towel. He was still trying to choke down the last chunk of pancake.

Stella patted him hard on the back as she poured him some more coffee and glared at the two puny guys at the other end of the table. "Keep the towel. I don't think the juvenile delinquents are finished yet." She placed the carafe on the island and retook her seat.

Manny's detective gene had kicked in, and he was now ignoring the side chatter. "How old did the bone look?"

Hooker yawned and blinked his eyes. He may have made it through the shower, but Manny could see he was still having trouble getting his right hand to work proficiently enough to get his usual clean, crisp shave around the tight thin beard framing his jaw. Manny knew Stella would quietly corner him later and clean up the wandering stubble.

Hooker grabbed his mug and sipped with one eye looking hard over the rim. He slowly lowered it. "I'm not a pathologist or an archeologist, nor do I play one on television, but the bone was light-colored in the dark and rain. If I had to guess, I would say it was very probably from this era —certainly not from the Paleolithic age." His mug returned to his face. Manny knew there was a self-satisfied grin behind the stoneware.

He thought through the whole idea of a random human bone showing up at the wreck. Then what would be the odds for two bones from different limbs? The odds were beyond Manny's advanced math, even though he loved to deal with those kinds of esoteric quantifiers on a crime scene. It was the vast and fast brain of his that had established him as the top detective in half the time it took for most to even get on the squad. It also didn't hurt to have a great partner.

Manny blinked slowly. Hooker knew the tattle-tale of his. This was the wind-up, and here comes the fastball, game-winning pitch.

"How soon will you be at the Fly's?"

Hooker looked at the Squirt then stood. Looking into the sunroom for his partner, he finished the conversation as he turned. "Box, go time." The orange streak skidded to a stop at the large front door as Hooker stepped over. "Shit." He had forgotten he was barefoot. The perfect exit was now just blown into the weeds and would burn there for weeks. Hooker opened the large door for the twenty pounds of cat. "Pee, and we'll be right with you." As an afterthought, he swung the door open again. "And leave

Mike alone. No beating up the poor mutt until he is at least two."

Hooker closed the door as he felt the Squirt scurry around behind him to retrieve his boots. As Hooker came out of his bedroom and headed for the door, he could hear Manny already at work in his office. His favorite weapon these days was the phone, and he was a crack marksman.

Hooker smiled as he heard Manny connect with his old partner and now a county supervisor over the different police departments, sheriff, and highway patrol. "Paul, Manny, we have a very delicate sticky situation here..."

Hooker started to close the giant front door but felt the Squirt's hand. They walked to the truck in silence. Each with his own thoughts for the day's agenda, Hooker looked to where his cat was standing straight-legged—splayed in the small patch of grass planted just for him.

The rest of the large expanse of apron and approach would be the size for a respectable filling station was all eight-inch thick concrete. The queen of this domain sat waiting in all of her yellow and blue splendor. The auto club colors, but the blue was shaded in a candy-apple, and the whole was shot over with pink and red mother-of-pearl. In the right light, the entire eleven tons would flash irides-cent neon red, making the fastest truck in the Bay Area look like it wasn't going to a fire, but was the fire itself.

"Box, go time." The streak bounced off the oversized fuel tank in front of Hooker's knee, ricocheted off the heat shield of the exhaust stack and in through the open door. Hooker knew he would hit his cardboard box, circle three times, and set his butt down so Hooker's right hand could reach his right ear to rub while the radios and engine warmed up. Box may be only a cat, but he was the smartest partner Hooker could ever want.

Hooker eyed the kid as they both climbed in. He smiled to himself. *Maybe a close second, but definitely a second.*

The Squirt buckled his belt. He thought about putting on the five-point harness but figured if Hooker wasn't moving fast, he wouldn't be driving fast, especially during the daylight, when cops could see him clearly. The Squirt looked over to see a small smile.

"What?"

Hooker shoved the small silver key in the keyhole and turned the beast on. He listened as the stators took hold and warmed the glow plugs. His electric drives slowly wound the turbochargers up to speed. The whine ran from low grumble to a climbing whine. Hooker always wondered if it must feel the same for a fighter in a jet plane. As the three sounds reached perfect harmony, Hooker briefly pushed the small magical silver button. Unlike other diesel trucks not babied and watched after by a fussing mother hen named Uncle Willie—the engine exploded into its new character-istic thrumming with a low-speed whistle.

The original engine in the 1959 Marmon had only been nine-hundred horsepower. Hooker and his Uncle Willie had built the original engine up to very respectable twelve-hundred horses. Earlier in the spring, Hooker had destroyed the engine while stopping a serial killer. The result of the day was Mae West, Hooker, and the Squirt had all been sidelined and needed rebuilding. Only the truck, Mae West, had come out ahead. In the rebuild, she had lost the archaic duel-transmission system with its twenty-four gears. She was refitted with a swifter set of sixteen gears driven by a now sixteen-hundred-horse engine originally, only the Department of Energy would have ever owned. Part of the new engine was the tattle-tale whistle.

Hooker's right hand dropped with the two fingers and thumb curled to engage the ear below. If the cardboard box ever moved, Box the cat would put it right back to its rightful place next to Hooker's seat. The ear was never out of place.

Hooker rolled his head to look at the Squirt as he listened for the engine noise to change. He never had to watch the pyrometer in order to know the temperature of his engine. With Hooker, it always was about felt and hearing the changes.

Hooker nodded his head up. "What?"

The Squirt smiled. He had long gotten used to the ritual of beginning the day with Hooker, Box, and Mae West. "You were smiling like there was something funny when you climbed in."

Hooker smiled as his hand rose to move the shifter. Floating it back and forth in the neutral line, he found his balance. Stomping on the clutch, he set the gears for fifth and eased off the apron and out onto the street, taking them down The Hill of Stupid. "I was just thinking about how smart Box is. He's not like any other cat or dog I have ever heard of, and I was just marveling at how lucky I was to get him as a partner."

The Squirt held his eye for a couple of heartbeats and then slewed them back out the front and over to his side as he checked along the working bed in the rearview mirror. He knew Hooker had not lied to him—he just had not shared everything. But the Squirt was satisfied with what he had gotten. The cat was something he too marveled at, and he was happy the twenty-something pounds of orange tabby was a friend instead of foe.

CHAPTER FOUR

To CALL THE Fly's an auto body shop is to call the Queen Mary a boat. The Fly's had six entrances on four different streets and a constantly used railhead. Hooker never used any, but the tow gate, which was a two-way river of steel, glass, and rubber. If it weighed more than three tons of unladen weight, the Fly's got it. If it was a Volkswagen with half of its original length, the Fly's got it. If Hooker towed it, and it wasn't going to a place of repair a club member designated, your insurance adjuster knew where it ended its life of usefulness.

Hooker parked Mae in his usual spot along the fence. Her size would be out of the way, but it was also along the main street of business for many mechanics and people who might need a tow. Even though they wouldn't require a truck as large as Mae, it was still good advertising.

The short Asian woman who everyone called Fly, but was actually not even related, spotted Hooker walking through the front door of the business office and called out,

"Hooker, you're late!" This was a standing joke among the many companies Hooker dealt with because if anything, Hooker was always early. Early to a wreck, early to get the pick of the crop, and early to get it delivered with the outside chance he might get two tows out of a wreck instead of one or none. This caused some grumbling among many of the other drivers who were not hustlers by nature, but it also created a lot of respect from the right sort of people. Fly was one of them.

"Jeez, Fly, cut me some slack." He waved his thumb over his shoulder in the direction he hoped the Squirt was still standing. "The Squirt took a while to figure out his toes went into the boots first... and then there was the whole question of the left or right thing."

If the woman came much above Hooker's belt buckle, she was wearing heels. She pursed her lips for a brief moment. "You brought me a dead bone, but it had a bone in it."

"I heard."

"It really a two-bit tow." She was referring to the two and a bit of dimes still floating around in not only Hooker but the Squirt, as well.

"Hey, Squirt was working on it too... that makes it a four-bit."

The woman who worked in the most testosterone-driven male industry grabbed near her crotch "I've got your four bits hanging right here. I think Dog is still out back in the morgue. He kept the bone for safekeeping. I didn't want somebody's ghost visiting the office and hanging around. I have enough of those of my own."

The woman stepped close to Hooker and looked up. "Don't look up; just look at me. Jessie is back there talking to the new girl, isn't he?"

Hooker nodded.

"He's been sleeping over at Mai Lin's apartment for the last few months." She hung her head, matching the hand holding a large wad of papers. "Where did I go wrong? I didn't raise my daughter to fall in love with slime buckets who cheat on her." She looked up with hope in her face. "You still single. Why don't you date her?"

Hooker put his hand on the small woman's shoulder. "I kind of like where my relationship with the Squirt's sister is going." He looked up at the body mechanic hunched over the desk and making time with some new skirt. "But just for you, I'll take care of this for you. Can you spare a mechanic?"

The Fly turned her large head of long hair done loosely in a mass bun held together with four chopsticks and a couple of pencils. She watched the subject of their discussion. Turning back, she sighed. "Just don't hurt him on my property. Otherwise, you can leave him out in the mudflats of Fremont for all I care."

"I'll go talk to Dog. That will give you enough time to get Jessie's check ready." Hooker smiled.

The Fly looked to see Hooker was serious. "On your way out, pull up by fuel dump and fill up on me."

Hooker warned her, "I'm running on less than twenty in my fourth tank."

"If you can make it stick and he leaves Mai Lin, you can fill up on me all month."

Hooker knew she would never say such a thing unless she was serious. She was known for making a nickel squeal like a dollar, but when it came time to pay for things, she bought quality, not cheap. He patted her on the shoulder as he walked past. "One step at a time, Fly, one step at a time." He didn't have to look back for the Squirt. He knew the kid was no more than six feet behind him.

The 'morgue' was where dead things ended up. People went to the one downtown while cars and trucks ended up in the large brown building near the railroad spur. There were always one or two rail cars waiting on the spur to be loaded with scrap steel. This was Dog's domain. Hooker wound his way through the large heaps of mangled auto and truck parts. He turned as a low whistle came out of the Squirt behind him. He nodded his head up at the kid, who had never seen this part of cars before.

"All of this is..."

"Scrap." Waving his hand about the basketball court-sized sorting area, Hooker explained, "This is about a week or two of sorting through wrecks. The parts that are still good are auctioned off to wrecking yards and used parts houses. The scrap metal is sorted by type and shipped out on the rail cars or sent to the crusher. Marmons become Macks and Peterbilts—they become Mopar, and after the metal has gone through Volkswagens and soup cans, they become Fords and Chevys." Hooker smiled evilly at the Squirt.

They turned and walked past two pallets of carburetors and another of shock absorbers. "Hooker, just the man I want to see."

Hooker and the Squirt turned to see the black man with Asian eyes. "Hey, Dog, what's hanging?"

"Two cheap shots and a crowbar for my date tonight. Who's the squirt?"

The Squirt hung his head. "Shit, we going to keep doing this stuff?" Hooker laughed. The poor kid had been nailed as the Squirt, a vernacular for *the new guy*, ever since he started being hauled around by Hooker during the spring.

"Dog, this is John. John, this is Dog." Hooker winked to the black man. "But he's getting used to the name Squirt. I think Dolly is embroidering "The Squirt" on his shirts." Hooker watched the kid turn even brighter red as he looked anywhere but at Hooker or Dog.

Hooker turned back to Dog. "You had a bone show up in the car?"

The man wheeled around on his one metal leg. "Not just a bone." He lumbered his way toward a bench that might pass for his office desk. "As I was hosing out the land-fill you decided I needed, I came across the hand and something else."

He bounced up against the large workbench. "I know you just love a good mystery, so here is your mystery for the month." He pulled an oil pan from a small straight engine down from the shelf and handed it to Hooker. "The watch was on the hand."

Hooker looked in the pan with the Squirt looking over his shoulder. Sure enough, there were the skeletal remains of a human hand and the main bone up to the elbow. A metal band watch was still on the bone. The gray-red clay from the area had tinted the bone along with age. To Hooker's untrained eye, the bones could be ten years old or a hundred and ten years old. Only the watch made it in the last thirty or forty years. Dog had carefully cleaned the gold watch.

"If you can't find out anything, I'd sure like the watch."

Hooker was sure Dog would rather he just forget anything about a mystery and hand over the watch right there. "Give me until summer, Dog. If I find nothing and if it's okay with the sheriff, then I'm sure it can be yours. After all, you found it and could have just kept your mouth shut and not told me anything." Hooker looked at the man.

"Jeez, Hooker, what kind of guy do you think I am?"

"An honest one."

"Damn right. The Fly trusted me the second day I was out of prison. I ain't never betrayed her trust. I don't plan to start a shit now."

Hooker stuck his hand out and shook the man's hand. "Let's keep playing it, Dog, just the way you've been. I'll tell you what, if I find a rightful owner and have to let it go, I'll buy you and a lady steaks at the Bold Knight. Deal?"

"We're good." They started to break the shake.

Hooker choked back onto the man's hand and leaned in close. As Hooker talked, the man listened, with a smile slowly spreading across his face.

Dog nodded. "You got it, boss. I'll make a couple of calls. It won't cost more than a six-pack or four."

Hooker nodded. "Don't forget about Fly's daughter."

The man drew back with a struck-smitten look. "Ain't no decent man in his right mind who ever met her can forget her."

Hooker studied the man hard. "If you get a shot at her—I think you would even have the Fly's blessing."

"Consider it done by the end of the day."

Hooker turned to leave. "I'll keep in touch, Dog."

"Thanks, Hooker, you're the best."

Hooker looked at his watch and hustled. "We need to fly out of here, Squirt. We are late for our dates."

The Squirt frowned. "Da... dates? What dates? You didn't tell me anything about..."

"On the chalkboard for over a week now, my young Squirt."

"What chalkboard?"

Hooker stepped up onto the truck and opened the door. Sliding the oil pan and body parts behind his seat, he climbed in and started the engine. Squirt clawed his way in the other side. "What chalkboard?"

"Already asked that, Squirt." Hooker cleared both directions of the street and nosed Mae West out on to San Jose Avenue heading east. He would wait on the fuel and make the fill-up worthwhile—instead of only three-quarters of one tank out of his four. The day was warm for being overcast, and it felt good to hang his arm out the window. Stopping at Monterey Highway, he turned south. Hooker leapfrogged the gears and rolled along to the highway at a quick clip. He glanced over at his passenger. "Really, you haven't been down to the mole hole to see your own sister in more than a couple of weeks?"

The apartment was in the lower level. It had been used as storage and a three-car garage. With events, Stella had turned one of the large storage areas into an apartment for

Candy, who was starting nursing school. The separation of one floor accessed by a secret set of stairs everyone knew and used was not lost on Hooker or Candy. Even though the apartment was built with two bedrooms, Hooker and the Squirt still floated between their two rooms in the Hacienda Romero and the two rooms at Uncle Willie's where they were headed at the moment.

"What does my sister and her apartment have to do with anything?"

"Just outside her apartment door is a new chalkboard. You might want to get familiar with it. You have some heavy dating scheduled on it."

"Dates?"

"Why does a date seem like such an alien concept to you?"

"I've never... I mean..."

Hooker swung his head in amazement. As he stared at the kid, his mouth hung open in mock shock.

The Squirt blushed and looked out his open window. "Oh, shut up."

Hooker almost made a teasing comment, but then stopped himself out of respect for the young man who had saved his life and paid dearly for it. "Dude, you're young. Besides, how would you take a girl out, the bus? You have years of dating. Let's see how today goes." Hooker smiled. "Besides, it's not like a regular date. This one you're getting naked for."

Hooker laughed at the horror-struck face. He knew he had hit the nail on the head.

CHAPTER FIVE

THE HILL UP to Uncle Willie's was only two downshifts. If Hooker wasn't taking it easy on the new engine, he could have just nailed the fuel and powered up the hill with only the single downshift at the bottom. He chuckled the whole way up the mile of hill as he listened to the new huge engine barely work. The hill was a quiet old neighborhood Willie had bought into in the late 1950s.

His property was at the end of the climb, and unlike the neighboring lots, was a full three acres dominated by a small house attached to what had started life as a hanger for a Navy blimp. The hanger was never built, and Willie had bought it for literally one cent on the original dollar. It came with full delivery, which Willie had nursed into full crection. Him having a great swimming pool and barbecue pit had the company of engineer Seabees milking the construction for the entire summer.

This didn't upset Willie one bit. In fact, he enjoyed

having a hundred young, good-looking hard-body sailors strutting their stuff shirtless and in his view. A view he had to deny himself to enjoy during the decades he worked as a Navy Intelligence officer. However, as a retired old captain, he was allowed his due.

Hooker nosed Mae up off the street and onto the approach apron to the gigantic door standing sixty feet high and almost forty feet wide. The door was made for walking combat blimps or weather balloons through unscathed. Something like the eleven tons of Mae West was like a pencil through a fist-sized knothole.

Squirt opened his door and slid out. "I've got this." He entered the little man door, and moments later, Hooker heard the large klaxon horn sound and watched the door slowly roll back. The electric motor was a GE hundred-horse motor originally tasked with pulling anchor chain on a light frigate. Willie didn't like the original forty-horse motor because it took almost a full minute to open the door the entire forty feet.

Hooker stuck Mae into third gear and just let his foot off the clutch. The power eased her forward at a slow walk as they traversed the depth of the two-hundred-foot-long auto shop. Willie was standing at the end of the grease pit and guided Hooker over the pit.

Hooker slid out as Mae shuddered the last throes of life. As Hooker's feet landed on warm concrete, Box bounced off his shoulder and was across the shop headed for the grass beyond. Hooker called out at the loping cat. "No beating up any dogs, Box. I want you to have a pure record for Santa this year." The cat slowed to a walk, glanced back in what

Hooker knew to be a glare, and continued out to at least use the grass.

Hooker shook his head as he turned and smiled at Uncle Willie. The man slumped down on one hip. His Navy flattop haircut never seemed to change. The large slash of a scar across his neck and up the side of his face was showing pinker today than the dead white of most days. Hooker chalked it up to the rose-colored paisley dress the man was wearing.

"Nice dress, Willie. You almost can't see the burn marks yet."

"Don't sweet talk me, young man. You know I won't be doing any welding this week." The man liked the feel of dresses. Also, it was, in his mind, justifiably economics. He bought the long granny dresses at Goodwill by the large garbage-bag full. He bought them at the going rate of rags and by the pound, which worked out in Willie's mind to less than twenty-five cents a dress. And they didn't burn up any faster than a pair of four-dollar bib overalls—when you could find any. They were frugal but with the benefit of also placating his 'Nancy' side, as well.

A low, slow wolf whistle preceded the Squirt.

Willie lost any sense of serious officiousness. His hip slung out as his face softened, and he turned to address the young man dressed in a mirror image of Hooker. "Well, John, it is so good to see a fine young man with at least some sense of taste and appreciation." He reached an arm out to solicit a hug. "You are looking and moving quite well for someone who, a short time ago, was half dead."

The young man didn't hesitate. His hug was strong and

true, which he brazenly finished with a kiss on the check. "And how is the best uncle on the east side doing? I really like the deep color of the paisley. It's certainly got the *go to town and raise hell* look about it." His smile was large and sincere.

Hooker quietly placed his palm on his face. "Oh, Gawd, please don't encourage him."

"Oh, hush yourself, Hooker. Just because you don't have any taste, don't be bad-mouthing another." Turning to Squirt and sliding his hand about his waist, he guided him toward the door to the house part of the building. "Why, John, you have slipped away to mere skin and bones. Let me see if there is anything Hanky left in the refrigerator I can fatten you up with." He leaned back and winked at Hooker as he nodded his head toward the darker southwest corner of the building.

Hooker glanced over to see the tan 1963 Dodge Dart convertible, commonly known in the family as The Granny Car. Hooker smiled as the car was now possessed by his girlfriend, and the Squirt's sister, Candy. He knew Willie was now leading a lamb to slaughter.

Candy and a fellow nursing student were there to earn hours toward the massage part of their schooling. Hooker was certain the Squirt, at twenty, had never had a massage. And now he knew the boy had never been really touched by a woman. The kid was now being led to his first of many therapeutic massages at the hands of his sister and fellow students.

Willie looked back just before they entered the door and gave Hooker a large, evil, lecherous smile. He was completely enjoying having a small but fun hand in the popping of the young boy's cherry, even if it was only a massage and for Willie, vicariously. Hooker knew that just the idea of the young kid naked under a sheet—being rubbed, was a visual thought the older man would carry for months.

As they entered the domicile through the steel fire door, they were greeted by three people sitting at the dining table. The two nursing students were talking quietly over tea with the swarthy older man. The thin white pencil-line mustache matched the same white at his temples and stood out boldly on the dark Greek.

Hank sat up and leaned back in his chair. "And so we have a lamb to slaughter." He spread his arms wide, which only enhanced his broad smile. "Hello, Squirt, welcome to a whole new world." He stood. "May I introduce you to your masseuse for the day, Cynthia? Cynthia, this is the Squirt, but for today, he's just a John."

Suddenly, the smile was shaken as Hooker and Willie started to laugh. "Oh, my, that did all come out wrong, didn't it?" The man flushed with embarrassment at the sexual innuendoes of both name and nickname.

The blonde stood with a soft, tinkling laugh. "It's okay, Hank. We all knew what you meant." She stuck her hand out toward the Squirt and parlayed her own innuendo. "I'm so glad to meet you, Squirt. Candy tells me you're a virgin... to being rubbed... massaged." Her smile and eye were steady as she viewed the score she landed on the young man only a couple of years younger than her.

Willie fanned his face with his hand. "Whew, is it hot in here or is it just all the sex talk?"

Candy, used to riding herd over errant men, took control. "We only have so much time." Standing, she touched Cynthia on the shoulder. "Why don't you get the Squirt undressed in the second bedroom, and I'll go get a hammer from the shop to use on Hooker."

Willie nosed up and over as he spun back toward the shop. "I think I'm going to go massage my girl now. A man in my delicate condition can only take so much pheromone at one time." He turned toward his partner. "The soup smells wonderful, Hanky. Don't forget to give me fair warning for lunch. I think Mae is going to get me very dirty today."

The quiet, slender man pursed his lips, driving the white line askew. "More like a dirty mind if I know you, and don't you dare get that grease and oil anywhere near this god-like body." The palms of his hands gently smoothed down his physique.

Willie sing-songed his way out the door with, "Promises, promises, my Hanky-panky."

The remaining man just wagged his head and gave a knowing eye toward Hooker. The other three laughed as Cynthia pulled the Squirt away to her lair. Candy noted the look in the younger woman's eyes. "Regulation massage, Cyn, regulation massage. And use the sheet."

"Yes, mother hen." The door closed on a giggle.

Candy turned on Hooker and poked him in the chest. "Same goes for you, buster."

CHAPTER SIX

THE SOUP WAS as good as the aroma permeating the house had advertised. There were contented tummies and bodies in the kitchen, and the conversation was sparse and quiet.

Hooker had watched Willie, who had been uncharacteristically distracted during the meal. Hooker had also noticed Hank stealing worried glances as well. Hooker rinsed his and Candy's dishes and placed them on the stack by the sink. Turning, he stepped over and placed his hand on his uncle's shoulder.

Willie nodded his head toward the empty seat and pointed.

As Hooker returned to his chair, Willie reached in his pants pocket. Hooker realized then his uncle had changed from the dress to pants and shirt sometime during the day. He was prepared to go somewhere.

"As I ministered to our baby today, I found some most

disturbing items." He glared at Hooker. "We will talk later about the disgusting Ford oil pan, as well as the bones." He laid the gold watch on the Formica and chrome dining table. Only Hooker and the Squirt recognized it from the morning.

Hooker wasn't sure where to start. Willie started for him. "This is a Rolex. Not just any Rolex. This is called a DateJust. It is written as two capitalized words but with no space between them. What the name means is that *just* as the hands reach midnight, the date changes. The metal band was invented by a company named Speidel. In 1947, they came out with this band called the Golden Knight. There are damn few Rolex watches with a Gold Knight band. In fact, I have only heard of one."

Willie glanced up at his partner and lover Hank, almost asking for the okay to continue. Returning his eyes to Hooker, he did. "Maddie and I had gone up to San Francisco to deliver a very fast car to a man who paid a high dollar for an untraceable car capable of outrunning anything on the road. We won't talk about how stupid he was by not paying attention to the highway patrol installing used military radios in their cruisers.

"So there we were, in San Francisco, with money burning in our pockets, and the train didn't come through until four the next morning. In those days, we didn't drink anything that didn't come from the end of a copper tube.

"Down on Market Street, there was a very nice jewelry store among the nice places to eat and just down from Saint Francis to sleep. In the window were these two items. We went in. I didn't need a watch as I was wearing whatever the Navy was giving me at the time. Maddie always wore her Cartier tank watch given to her grandmother for her grandfather's service in the Tank Corps that liberated France in The Great War. But her oldest brother had broken his watch during D-Day on Omaha beach."

Willie dabbed at the side of his eyes. The memory was as fresh as yesterday. "We went off to a long dinner while the jeweler engraved the back of the watch." He rolled the now carefully cleaned watch inside out and handed it to Hooker.

Engraved in a fine bookplate font were the words, *To My Golden Knight Brother Danny. Love, Your Little Rocket Sister, Maddie.*

The watch became very heavy in Hooker's hand, as the universe grew dark. He handed it to Candy, who read it and handed it to the Squirt. All three knew exactly who Maddie was and who she was to Willie.

The Squirt passed it back to Willie.

Willie mouthed a silent *thank-you.* He quietly stared at the engraving. He gathered the rest of his thoughts.

"When Korea started, he was still attached to the Army National Guard. But because of his field commission in France, and the few community college courses he took, they dragged him back in.

"In 1953, the letters stopped coming, but no Army pukes showed up at the door to do Honor Duty. Eventually, two MPs showed up looking for Danny. According to them, he had been shipped to San Francisco's Letterman Hospital, but never showed up."

The man just stopped. There was no more. It was now

Hooker's turn.

"The other night, some lady slid her Caddie off the edge on the Snake. The gully there is about a hundred feet, but she didn't do so bad. She went down ass first, and so her head banged on those new headrests. It took her about three hours to walk out to the Cats and a payphone. I guess Rollie went in first but knew his ton and a half would flip trying to pull the de Ville out. So I was called in. I found a leg bone and just flipped it aside. But, when I dragged the Caddy up, it must have scooped the side of the hill, and I guess it caught this. There was a lot of mud in the car, and when Dog over at the Fly's washed it out, he found the hand and this watch."

Willie rubbed his upper lip between his thumb and forefinger as he thought. He looked up at Hooker.

"Is Mae ready?"

Willie nodded.

Hooker stood and reached for the phone on the wall. He dialed without really looking at the numbers. "Hi, Karen. It's Hooker. Listen, when Dolly..." He rolled his eyes. "Yes, ma'am. Yes, ma'am. I was there already this morning. Yes, ma'am, I could see how it would upset some people. Yes, ma'am. Yes, ma'am. We just finished a little pow-wow here with Willie. The Squirt and I are going out to look around."

Hooker looked at Willie and nodded. He turned his attention back toward the phone. "Yes, ma'am. We'll meet him at the downside of the Cats. Yes, ma'am. I love you, too." He hung up and turned. The two young ladies were relaxed back in their chairs and smiling. Willie was close to laughing. Only the Squirt had a solemn look on his face.

Willie broke. "Is Dolly feeling a little mother hen needy this morning?" Dolly's day, like Hooker's, usually started around five in the evening. This was mid-afternoon, and she was already in her custom-built stainless-steel desk chair to accommodate her quarter-ton of flesh for running the city by night. A large limb lay on her desk within arm's reach. Carved into it were the words 'The Stick.' It was Dolly's to touch and use, and nobody else. It was what she used to stir the shit up with, and if she was in her desk a few hours early —there was shit flying from somewhere.

"The Fly called. Someone saw the bones Dog washed out of the car and called the PD. They came down. Dog told them it wasn't any of their business. I need to go make nice and get him out of jail. The Fly will post the bond, but the truth is the Snake isn't PD's area. So Dog was right."

"What about the highway patrol?"

"It was Micha who called me and worked the scene, but I think it was just because the woman had called from the Cats. Highway 17 is theirs, but the Snake would be more like the unincorporated area and come under the Sheriff." Willie and the Squirt booth groaned.

Willie asked, "Who are you meeting at the Cats?"

"Chet. I guess so we can go down and pop Dog out, and Chet can drive his flag into the investigation before this turns into a three-ring cluster..." Willie gave Hooker a stern look.

"There *are* ladies present."

"We'll just be leaving then. Squirt?"

The Squirt got up and shook Cynthia's hand. "Thank you for the great massage. I never knew it could feel so good."

Cynthia smiled. "I'll look forward to the next time I get you on a bed."

Candy pulled down her nose with thumb and forefinger as she looked at the other woman. There was just a hint of more than a message lurking in the smile. Maybe she had to watch whom she chose to join in on massaging the recovering hero.

Hooker bent over and kissed the top of Willie's head as the man flipped his hand at him. He blushed slightly but still smiled. Hooker gave a quick smooch at Candy, and then the two young men grabbed their matching leather jackets and donned them over their matching starched white T-shirts over matching jeans and boots. The girls giggled, but Willie saw the man of today and the man who he once had been.

The steel fire door closed solid.

They could hear Hooker yell for Box, and then the giant truck roared into life and shook the building. Candy glanced over at Willie. The man had a very satisfied, warm look on his face. He was comfortable in the life that had come to grace him.

Hank came in through the almost never used front door. "I have some good cilantro and chives. The rosemary just hasn't done well in the spot by the hose bib. But I think I can make do on the tri-tip tonight. Ladies, can you stay for dinner? There is plenty for six."

Hank stopped and counted the heads and then heard the distinct sound of Mae West as Hooker shifted for the top of the hill and the subsequent drop. "Well, I guess it just means more for four." The man smiled and danced his way toward the sink as he waved his pom-poms of herbs.

CHAPTER SEVEN

D OWN ON THE freeway, the eleven tons of yellow and blue steel monster was just warming up as Hooker flipped the toggle and plunged the shifter into ninth gear. He dropped the hammer and signaled into the second lane and blew past the Pontiac Firebird. The late afternoon was holding steady at cool but was always warm enough for two leather elbows out the windows. The French vanilla triple scoops of ice cream would wait until after midnight.

Hooker reached behind his head to grab the microphone off its perch. This was the personal radio, usually only going to the credenza behind Dolly. Only occasionally, after midnight, it reached out to a small version at a local radio station. The latter was for communication with one of the more bizarre lines of communication for solving problems or watching for upcoming problems.

Sweets was the night disk jockey and worked the midnight to six o'clock shift. When his sight was taken from him by a freak accident in his high school welding class, his visual sight was replaced by a sixth sense. He didn't always know what he was looking at, but he did know who it was meant for. More times than Hooker cared to remember, this sixth sense had been his protection or help in figuring out a problem.

Sweets' brother, Danny, a former lineman for USC until the accident, was now his chauffeur and protector. Danny wouldn't have it any other way.

During Hooker's recovery from the surgeries to remove the dimes a killer had left in him and the Squirt, Danny had studied texts to help in Hooker's physical therapy. The giant black man and the younger Hooker had become fast friends. Hooker knew Danny would lay down his life for Sweets and their mother and suspected he would do the same for Hooker as well.

Hooker toggled the side switch and called the woman who would qualify as his first mother behind her sister Stella. "1-4-1."

The pause didn't last more than a heartbeat. "Go ahead, Hooker."

"Do you know if Chet is in his cruiser with a radio?"

"Stand by one."

Hooker looked over at the Squirt and nodded a raised eyebrow shrug. With the mic still in his hand, he reached down and shifted down a gear.

"10-4, honey. What do you need?"

"Why not have him meet us at the jail. It will save the backtrack time."

There was a pause, and then Karen's voice took over for

Dolly. "Chet says to meet him at the Whole Doughnut. He can leave the cruiser there."

Hooker laughed. "He doesn't need a doughnut in his condition. He needs to start running again. I'll be 10-97 in ten minutes."

"10-4. Dispatch out."

Hooker dropped one more gear, hung up the mic, and dropped two more as he nosed the truck into the winder cloverleaf from the 101 to the 280. They passed under the floating pieces of a future overpass everyone referred to as the Altars to Stupidity. Under Governor Reagan, the state had prospered, and many infrastructure projects were started. With the election of Jerry 'Moonbeam' Brown, the twenty-billion-dollar emergency fund for disasters had evaporated on the state's way toward bankruptcy within the year. Any and every project was stopped. So the altars stood, rotting and unfinished.

Hooker looked over at the Squirt, who was staring numbly out the window. Quietly, Hooker laughed to himself. He had seen the look before... in the mirror. He stomped on the go pedal and jumped back up the three lost gears and settled out with one extra.

"Still thinking about the massage?"

The Squirt drifted back into the cab and turned toward Hooker. He turned in the seat so his legs were in the middle, and his back was leaning against the door. The wind in the window tossed the hair on the back of his head. In a drifting but analytical voice, he reviewed the event. "Yeah... I think. First, if she's going to touch me... umm..."

"Intimately?" Hooker smiled as he glanced over.

"Yeah, intimate. So why cover you with the sheet?"

"Did you have sex?"

The kid blushed but was shocked. "No. Nothing like that..."

"Did she touch your pecker?"

"No..." John was now frowning at Hooker, who seemed to be getting a little too personal.

"But she rubbed your butt." The Squirt nodded. "And you weren't cold."

Hooker had to look over at the now silent kid. John was only twenty and had experienced a lot, but not much was nice to him.

"I think it's the law, but the sheet serves many purposes. It keeps you warm, it gives you a sense of privacy even when she's rubbing really near your hoo-hoo, but most importantly, it reminds both of you that you are there for a massage, not sex."

The kid smiled at the information. Then he decided to push the envelope with the one person who he knew it was safe to do it. "What if she is willing to—"

Hooker stopped him "Then you better negotiate it for another time. If it was to happen, she would most likely get thrown out of the program as unprofessional."

"So this would be okay?" The kid held up a small piece of paper Hooker knew probably had a phone number written on it.

"You're learning, John." He shook his head and smiled as he downshifted to take the off-ramp. "You are certainly learning." For some reason, calling him Squirt at the moment didn't seem right.

The kid turned back around as he stashed the number in his jeans. "She said with the extent of my injuries and surgeries that I would probably need a lot of extra care." His smile was more self-satisfied than just a massage would put there.

Hooker smiled as he pulled the large white Bakelite steering wheel around to make the turn at the top of the ramp. Jamming the shifter into neutral, he toggled down to the next set of gears and pulled it back into what was now sixth gear. The thought drifted warmly across his mind, *yeah, that's what your sister told me, too.*

A short romp down the Guadeloupe Parkway and Hooker nosed Mae into the back parking lot behind the most popular doughnut place in town, The Whole Doughnut. As he set the air brakes, he heard the wooden screen door snap shut, bouncing a couple of times.

The high voice was English, with a lot of Vietnamese accents thrown in. "Why you come now, Hooker? You know missy Stella in town. My God Father, no can have cherry-filled doughnuts unless she go away."

Hooker laughed as he eased the door open and slid out for a hug. "I know, Mai Lin, but some days, the hardworking tow driver just needs something sweet... like a hug." He enveloped the small woman as he waved toward her husband, Ralph.

Ralph had fallen in love with Mai Lin in Vietnam. When he was pulled out, he told his commander they had gotten married, and she was pregnant with their child. The commander looked at the blown up soldier and to the then fifteen-year-old Mai Lin. He figured if she would have the beat-up half a man, and he was willing to take her home, who was he to come between the two?

Convincing the State Department was another matter. Eventually, it came to light that they weren't married, and Mai was not eighteen. Everything was in limbo while Ralph sat in one cell and Mai Lin in another. It was getting heated around the police department as they wanted nothing to do with the State Department or immigration problem. To make matters worse, while Ralph was in jail, the Army showed up with some medals he was due.

Manny was sitting in the office and heard the whole story from beginning to end. His only question for the State Department guy was what needed to happen to make sure she wasn't shipped back. There were only two things available considering her age—sponsorship and or adoption.

Manny told the guy to go to lunch, and then he walked down the hall to have a long talk with Mai Lin. By the time the guy came back from lunch, Manny had one of the County Clerks draw up emergency papers of foster care pending adoption, as well as a judge's signature and registered stamp. Manny sent the State Department guy packing, and the two love birds were released into his care.

He checked them into a motel up the peninsula and convinced an old friend he needed two new employees willing to work for free for a month or so. They learned everything the doughnut house had to offer, including how to treat the cops. While they were learning the business, Manny was finding them the right location, as well as taking donations from every cop, detective, street worker, fireman, or city employee who may ever chance to eat a doughnut.

The 'Whole' stood quite literally for the whole of city workers having a piece of interest in it becoming a success. The two kids opened to a daily sell-out, and they had been working hard ever since. The day Mai Lin turned eighteen was the day Manny walked her down the aisle and gave her over to Ralph. The two had been worshiping each other ever since.

"How's it hanging, Hooker?" Ralph sauntered up in his broken gait with the obligatory unfiltered cigarette hanging from his lips. He put his hand out. Hooker took it and was always amazed at the mass of scar tissue hiding a grip of steel coming from the man kneading hundreds of pounds of dough each day.

"You know, Ralph, just another day in paradise looking for something to choke down."

John had finished checking all the tires and walked up.

Ralph nodded his way and started to ask Hooker a question. John cut him off and offered out his hand. "Hi, the name is John, but everyone calls me Squirt."

Mai Lin laughed and waved her hand as she returned to the back door. The screen door slammed and then squealed back open. "Hey, Mister Squirt, what kind doughnuts you like?"

John looked at Hooker, who just shrugged. The Squirt turned, "I like the kind you choose for me."

Ralph laughed and looked at Hooker as he nodded at the Squirt. "He's going to go a long way, this one." Giving the Squirt a mock glare, he advised, "Easy on the hormones, soldier—she's my boss, and she's married."

Hooker snorted and nodded toward the Squirt. "In the

spring, if he's physically able, he starts at the police academy."

Ralph's eyes lit up. The face and name finally hit home. "So you're the two-bit guy who saved Hooker's ass?"

The voice was deep and raspy. "Yes, he did—as well as putting the psycho where they belonged." The Highway Patrol Captain walked around the back end of the truck. "But before he shot her, he figured out things that broke the case." Chet put out his hand to the kid. "Good to see you up and walking around, Squirt."

"Always a pleasure to see you too, Captain." The kid beamed as they shook hands.

The screen door squealed and snapped shut. "I see you drive in, Captain. You have chocolate bar, Hooker has frog, and Squirt has two éclairs because he growing boy." Mai Lin presented the bag to the Squirt. "You guard so they don't steal your food."

The men all laughed at the obvious fondness and favoritism the small woman delivered with the heart of a tiger. Hooker and the Squirt collected their hugs and headed for Mae West, lumbering as if she were a large ticking clock.

Chet opened his arms. Mai looked sternly at him. "You no get hug. You no come see Mai enough. Mai tell you to take care of yourself." She waved her right hand up and down at the man's body. "You no mind Mai. You just stand and be target for crazy person. You retire. Then you get hugs from Mai. Mai no like man with holes in him." She crabbed over and put her arm around Ralph. "Except maybe husband." She smiled.

Chet, defeated, headed for the truck.

As Hooker drove between eating the messy doughnut called a frog, they talked strategy.

"You know they aren't just going to roll over on this and give away a juicy case."

Chet popped the last of his doughnut into his mouth and shoved it into his cheek. "Sure they will after I point out a few things. One, we have jurisdiction and two, the case is at least four decades cold—"

"Two. We know who—"

"Hush, I'm talking. And don't you dare tell them anything about the watch. But the most important thing is, even Dog doesn't know where the car went over on the Snake. Only Micha can make a positive identification as to the location."

Hooker looked at Chet. "But the Squirt and I—"

"Didn't I just tell you to hush?"

Hooker rolled his eyes and downshifted with a smile. "Right, it was a dark and stormy night. If not for the highway crew, Mae and I would have been lost." Hooker sang to the tune of *Gilligan's Island*.

The Squirt chimed in, "And they would be lost on a three-hour tow, a three-hour tow."

Chet hung his head. "Oh, Gawd, there's now two of them."

Twenty minutes later, the Gilligan crew was squared off across the table with the police. The negotiations were stalled as the police chief was under the gun by the commissioner. He said he didn't care how old the case was, and the

PD needed a good, juicy case to play well in the Mercury News.

Finally, Hooker pushed back his chair and stood. All eyes were on him. "You'll have to excuse me for a few minutes." He looked at his watch. "It's after four. I need to call Commissioner Paul before I talk to Dolly at Dispatch." Everyone at the table knew Paul was Manny's ex-partner and still best of friends if not the same with Hooker. The mention of Dolly was enough to cause all four assholes to clinch shut on the PD side of the table.

Chet stood. "While you do that, I think I'll call out to Manny and ask how he's doing on the little project we talked about this morning."

The Squirt cleared his throat. Nobody expected he would have anything to contribute. Quietly, he looked the chief in the eye. "I know when you made me the offer to join your department after the shooting, you thought you were the only name in the game. But if this is the kind of pissing match that goes on here, I seriously may just have to take up the offer by San Francisco." He sat with an impassive stone face. He waited out the chief, unblinking.

Hooker paused and looked at the Squirt. The kid was no kid at the moment. "When did you get the letter?"

The Squirt never blinked. His stare was burning its way into the chief. "Last month, while Hooker was taking care of the other serial killer in your jurisdiction." The final shiv sunk home. The chief was outgunned by these two who had ended the reign of terror by not one but two separate serial killers in one year. And they had almost lost their lives in doing it: no medals, no ceremonies, no publicity. Two private citizens who did the job his department should have been able to do and hadn't.

The chief blinked. "Crap. But keep me in the loop."

Hooker was there for one thing and one thing only. "And Dog?"

The chief waved his hand backward. "Yeah, kick him loose."

Hooker pressed. "You have him on probation for another six months on a bogus DUI charge..."

The chief looked at Chet.

Chet smirked. "Welcome to the big leagues, Phil."

"Who was he arraigned under?"

"Stone."

"Oh, great. Swing 'em High Stone. Okay, I'll work it out with the DA."

Hooker knew when to close and be magnanimous. "Thank you, sir." He turned to the Squirt with a wink the PD side couldn't see. "Come on, Squirt, the Box needs to use the large lawn out here."

Neither spoke or smiled as they made their way down to lock-up and released Dog. It wasn't until they had all piled into the truck and were nosing out onto the street they finally spoke.

Hooker looked over at the Squirt "That was some great bullshit about San Francisco."

The Squirt just kept looking forward. The silence was thick.

Chet was the first to understand. "Who else did you get a letter from, son?"

The Squirt was quiet, gathering his thoughts. "Five on

the peninsula, three from Contra Costa County, four from Marin County, as well as the Sheriff of Los Angeles County." He turned to look with a small smile at Chet. "I'm still leaning toward the highway patrol. They have better cars, but the uniforms suck."

They were still laughing as they dropped Dog off at the Fly's and filled the fuel tanks.

The Fly had come out to greet them, and the usually hard edge was gone. She walked right into Hooker's unsuspecting middle and hugged him firmly. "I don't know how you did it, but that asshole Steve flew out of here without his check and was gone from my daughter's life within an hour."

Hooker looked at a retreating Dog, who had his palms up. "You don't have to share the hug, Hooker... I'll get one somewhere else." The man laughed and turned on his metal leg and walked back to work.

The Fly watched him go as her arms were still around Hooker. She wasn't sure what had just happened, but she liked the excuse to hug one of the special people in her life.

"Fly, I think you just might have swapped an asshole for a really nice guy who works hard—and worships your daughter for the great person she is. If you end up with Dog for a son-in-law, I think you will all win."

The small woman looked for any joking in Hooker's face. Finding none, she buried her face back into his tummy. The hug was almost painful.

Hooker hadn't been joking about his fuel level. He took over three-hundred gallons in his four tanks. For Hooker, he was running on fumes.

Hooker reached behind his head and grabbed the mic. "1-4-1."

Dolly's smooth voice oozed out of the speakers. "Ooo, I just love hearing from my three favorite juvenile delinquents. Can any of you three spare a girl a dime?"

Hooker remembered Chet also possessed a dime floating in his body the surgeons didn't want to try to remove. "We have four and a half bits, how much do you need?"

"Just what you can spare, honey. Now, what do you need? I'm busy here, knitting a pair of booties before the kid over there becomes a stupid tow truck driver."

Hooker held his laughter at the thought of Dolly trying to knit. "Can you see if Micha is on duty yet, please?"

"Stand by one."

They waited while someone tried the radio on the highway patrol network or called the substation. Hooker loafed Mae down Winchester Boulevard. If they could get him, it would make it easier to find the crash site again. He had been there in daylight hours and then guided Hooker back in the dark.

"He says he will take Chet on tack three."

"10-4, mama."

The Squirt fished his hand under the dash near where the illegal radio used to hide.

Hooker smiled. "Maddie upgraded the whole shebang." He reached overhead and toggled a red bat-switch that now glowed. Hooker grabbed the third mic hanging under the dashboard and handed it to Chet.

Chet held it waiting for the radio to warm up, but

Micha had other plans. "P-twelve to C-one." Chet looked hard at Hooker.

Hooker smiled as he nodded at the radio. "Don't get your panties in a twist. It came out of an Orion P-3 Sub Chaser out at Moffitt Field. Maddie just did some tweaking and upgraded it."

Chet's look was doubtful, but he keyed the mic. "C-one, go."

"What do you need?"

"What's your twenty?"

"I heard someone was headed for the Snake. I'm having some fine coffee and looking at two large cats."

Hooker nodded. "Fifteen." He eased down on the gas, took a right onto Hamilton Avenue, and readied for his favorite down-spiraling winder on-ramp.

"10-4, P-twelve. Give us fifteen."

Chet pitched the mic over to the Squirt—who had a seat belt on—as he braced himself in the opening to the sleeper. He had never ridden with Hooker, but he knew the young man's reputation for driving the largest tow truck like it was a sports car.

Hooker's reputation was no exaggeration. He had jumped up five more gears before the winder dumped him out onto the freeway at eighty miles an hour. Chet sat back in the sleeper and just shook his head. "I'm definitely not seeing this." Hooker knew that with Micha at the Cats, there was no other highway patrol on the weekend freeway.

CHAPTER EIGHT

THE SNAKE HAD dried out some since the night before. Hooker thought of the few moonshine runners still using it. They would enjoy a break in the fall weather as they conducted business during the holidays supplying the South Bay Area.

Most people thought of moonshine and runners as something from prohibition or the thirties. Hooker knew from being around Maddie that her family's main source of income was not from building and racing fast cars. It came from building fast street cars with large stainless-steel tanks with remotely triggered dumping ports. Willie once told Hooker a good dump could put over one hundred gallons of shine on the highway in the time it took to pull over and stop on the side of the road—about two blocks. Hooker had Maddie's brother put two hundred gallons on the highway in less than a hundred yards or three seconds. Pressurizing the tanks had revolutionized the process and the amount carried at one time. A back seat in a Lincoln Town Car might be nothing more than the thin leather glued over a handcrafted tank. The added ton of liquid was offset by suspension from a truck. Top to bottom, Maddie's family was creative and full of talent.

The highway patrol cruiser pulled off to the side of the road. As Hooker nosed Mae up to the rear end, the tall black officer eased out of the door. The fast draw smile was one of Hooker's favorites to see at a wreck, a bar, Dolly's Wednesday night's dinner table, or anywhere else they would run into each other. Their history ran deep into the days that Hooker was towing on a bogus driver's license, saying he was nineteen. Micha had never asked how old he really was the night in the rain when they had watched a prom queen of seventeen die in Hooker's arms.

The two met and shook with grim smiles. Nothing needed to be said. This meeting was never happening, and they weren't digging up old bones. It helped that Micha's boss walked up, holding out an extra pair of overalls. "Sorry, there weren't any more rubbers." Chet smiled.

Micha looked down at his boss's ratty running shoes and paint-splattered pants. "Getting some work done around the house for the holidays, I see." The two laughed at the old department joke. One year, Chet had worked long days until December twenty-sixth, and then, to surprise his wife, bought a tree already trimmed and being thrown out by a store. Snuck it home and plugged it in. The look on his wife's face made it the best five bucks he had ever spent. The small diamond ring had only helped. Cops don't get time for holidays.

They both knew Chet being sidelined due to reoccurring massive headaches since the shooting was eating at his insides. This holiday season was no happy time for Chet—with no work and his wife passing away a few years before. "I thought I'd finally get those dime holes plugged in the living room. I even got the window replaced last week."

The Squirt strolled past with the two shovels. "You two can supervise from up here where it's not so muddy or come join in the fun." They noted from the kid's deadpan delivery he was fully aware of what they would be digging up.

Except none of them were ready for what they would find.

The small sluice of rainwater from the night before had removed a lot of the loose mud and even more of the dirt wall of the hillside. As the other three finally climbed down, they found Hooker looking over the area with his flashlight. Two arm and hand bones stuck out from the cliff.

The count was not lost on the Squirt. "Oh, crap. There is more than just Danny."

"What the hell do you think happened here?"

Hooker shook his head toward Chet. "Hell if I know, but it wasn't good." He aimed his light on what might have been some yellow cloth.

Micha kneeled and dug around it with his hands. With little work, a large basketball-sized yellowish rubberized bag rolled out into his lap. "It's a waterproof dive bag. What the hell is it doing here?" He opened it and stuck his hand in. His face swung toward the others, and it wasn't good. His hand withdrew a small cup or bowl made from what looked like tarnished gold. There were markings engraved in the metal.

Chet leaned in with his flashlight. He had seen the markings before. "Oh, crap. Those are Egyptian, like the King Tut and Mummy stuff." He settled down in a squat to think. Turning to Hooker, he looked for some guidance. Hooker shrugged, knowing they were in way over his head. They had just clandestinely disturbed a crime scene, but they didn't know what the crime was.

Hooker squinted down his face as he rubbed it with his thumb and forefinger, searching for answers. Of the four men, Hooker had the most experience walking the other side of the line of the law. The two plus one future men of the law looked to him as a leader on this.

Hooker walked back over to the bushes and tree line, where he had noticed the old upside-down car rusting into oblivion. The years of rust had taken its toll on the steel. As he played his flashlight over the brown hulk, he could tell one of the doors had been open but was now crushed along with the rest of the top by the weight of the body. He knelt down and tried to see inside. The mice and other local denizens had chewed and nested the leathers, clothes, and stuffing of the interior. Rust was working on everything else.

He stood. "Hey Squirt, let's get a line down here and flip this."

The kid walked down to the access point that was easier to climb up. A few minutes later, the line and J-hook were tumbling down the hill with Hooker's unique roller chain attached.

Hooker pulled the rigging over to the car hulk and let out a sharp whistle. The line stopped feeding.

Hooker rigged the roller chain on the few areas he thought might be still strong enough to turn the car over. Short of a net and crane, Hooker knew the hulk would never leave the ravine. Pulling on the line, he gave two short whistles. The line started taking up slack slowly. The chains dug into the rotted metal but held. Gently, the hulk slewed around to square and then slowly rolled over. As it neared the tipping point, Hooker whistled a short sharp whistle.

The metal cadaver crashed onto its frame with rotted tires and wheels. The mass didn't even rock. The roll had crushed it even more. Hooker unhooked the chains and hook, and then whistled a long call for the Squirt to haul it away.

A few minutes later, as Hooker and Chet examined where the vehicle identification number should have been in the dashboard, the Squirt slid down and walked over. "Wow... that made quick work of this prom queen." Micha gave him a questioning look and realized the kid was probably let in on Hooker and his experience.

The other two were looking at a slotted hole where a plate with a long series of numbers should have been—instead of Hooker's hand. "Without the VIN, we can't trace whose car this was."

Chet started toward the driver's door, thinking of the more modern cars. Micha shook his head. "It won't be there on this car. My guess is this is pre-1940s. They didn't put the metal sticker on until after the Korean War."

Hooker grabbed the end of the hood and pulled. The Squirt saw him struggling and jumped to the other side. Soon, all four were lifting, and the rust finally gave away. With the hood up and where Hooker had hoped for an engine number, he only swore.

"What?" Micha echoed the Squirt.

Chet nodded at the engine. "It's a Lincoln straight-eight..."

Hooker finished. "And this is no Lincoln. I'll bet there is an extra tank back there where the back seat used to be, and it's made of copper. This was a moonshine runner. There won't even be any numbers on the engine. They were etched off with acid."

Micha looked at Hooker with a drawn face and one raised eyebrow. "Why, Hooker... it is amazing the things you know." He smiled.

The Squirt laughed. "Yeah, Maddie would be so proud of you."

Chet harrumphed. "Who do you think he learned it all from?"

Hooker wasn't laughing. "And it's who we are here for." Reminding Squirt, but not ready to share about the watch.

Hooker walked to the dry streambed and looked across at the cliff in the dark. The bones shone dully in the moonlight, but the night just seemed so wrong for the respect this job deserved. Hooker turned to where Chet had walked up behind him.

Chet, with a sober face, nodded. "We have four days without rain. How about we start early tomorrow?"

"What about the bag of stuff?"

Chet waved his head over his shoulder. "Throw it in the trunk of the wreck if we can get it open. Who's coming down here in the next few days besides us?"

Hooker looked at his watch with his light. He looked over at the Squirt talking to Micha as they leaned against the rusty hulk, and then back at Chet. "I can probably get in a tow or two also before we shut it down early enough to get the kid some rest."

Chet smiled, knowing both young guys still needed sleep to recover. "Let's get the trunk open."

As the two vehicles reached the end of the Snake, Micha turned west to go get some clean uniform pants and to clean his boots. Hooker jumped up onto the freeway and took the 17 back into San Jose and dropped Chet off.

Grabbing the mic from behind his head, he keyed the red switch twice.

Dolly's voice was almost instant in response. "I have a Peterbilt sitting on Polk Street in San Francisco. It needs to come down to the Fly. SFPD says they will probably be ready to release it in about an hour or two."

Hooker looked at the Squirt, who was making duck lips and nodding with smiling eyes. Long ride and easy money. The night didn't get much better.

"Is there a trailer?"

"Just the rig."

"Just need the cross street, sweetheart."

The Squirt nodded at the street name and turned toward Hooker. "I guess Togo's is closed at this hour."

Hooker smacked his lips like he had eaten something nasty. "Closed and your sister isn't working at the diner anymore. If it was near midnight, I'd swing by and say hi to Peter, but the pig they replaced Candy with ran everyone else off."

The Squirt chuckled. "Do you think we could get away with parking Mae out in front of Sam Woo's?"

"What do you know about Sam Woo's?" Hooker frowned as he upshifted. The kid just kept amazing him with the things he knew or was learning.

"One of the nurses at the hospital said she had her best experience there."

They both laughed. "Was she talking about the food or a Chinese guy?"

The big yellow truck swung north on the 101 freeway. With two elbows encased in black leather sticking out of the windows, an eerie blue glow underneath, and yellow lights in the wheel wells—Mae West dissolved into the night.

CHAPTER NINE

THE DIGGING WAS slow and careful as the men took turns excavating the bones. They tried to dig out each skeleton one at a time so they could keep them separate. Packed in and around the legs were three—once yellow diver's bags. One had broken, and some jewelry had spilled out into the cavity.

"There's another bag here, but the top was open when it was stuffed in." The Squirt pulled it free. "Or it looks like maybe there was a tear or something. Either way, some of this is stuff is loose." The kid moved slowly with a whisk broom from the working bed of Mae. It was hard for these amateur archeologists to know what to bring. So, for the most part, the four shovels stood unused, as the small gardening trowel seemed to get the most use, along with a small hand broom.

The canopy and folding table was the base of operations for packing the four body bags. The skeletons had almost no connections left due to the twenty years of wet soil to rot the flesh and a premium breeding ground for bugs crawling about in the earth and eating the flesh. Only once did Chet start humming and then realized he was voicing the old nursery rhyme of worms and playing cards on one's nose. He looked at the others who understood but showed no signs of humor. The day's work wasn't just another wreck in the night, where gallows humor was one of the common ways of dealing with the seemingly daily carnage.

Micha stood at the table where he and Hooker had just carried the hips to shoulders, one arm, and most of the other. He pointed at the missing left arm from the elbow down. "What do you think?"

"Maybe. Looks about right. Willie said Danny was about six-foot-two or so. This table is sixty inches..."

He was cut short by the Squirt's short bark in the hole. He crawled back out with a skull and part of a chain that should have had dog tags attached. "I think we have Maddie's brother." He walked over and gently placed the skull on the table. Handing the chain to Hooker, he said, "I think you're the one to hold on to this for now. Hopefully, we will also find the tags to go with it."

Hooker nodded and started to shove the partial chain in the chest pocket of his overalls. He dropped them into his left hand and reached back in for the shining thing he had picked up the night of the tow. Rubbing the item on his pant leg to clean it, he held it out.

His palm was almost covered with a large beetle. The statuette weighed almost a pound and appeared to be almost all out of gold. Micha was the first to break his fascination. "It's called a scarab. This would probably date back to the age of King Tut, or at least, Cleopatra."

The other three looked at the officer they actually only knew from work for the most part. Hooker asked, "You study this stuff?"

"Not really, just pick up a book here or there. There is a great museum over in Santa Clara; it has all of this kind of stuff. The wife likes museums, and it's a nice, quiet place to go."

Chet raised one eye and thought. "Is that the Rosicrucian Museum?"

Micha nodded, and Chet's face cleared. "My wife asked me a few times to go with her, but we never did." The regret was written on his face. He had adored his wife, but she was gone before they had done everything they wanted to do.

"I wonder if it's where this all came from?" Hooker mused. "I mean, we haven't looked at all of the stuff, but if it is all Egypt stuff..."

Chet rested his hand on the skeleton. "Let's square Danny away here, and then we have the table to take a look."

The two body bags lay in the shade, almost as if they were empty. Micha had brought some evidence tags, and they marked what they knew of each. Danny's had his name.

The table was soon filled with bowls, urns, jewelry, breastplates, armbands, small boxes, rings, and other gold jewelry. Almost nothing had jewels. Most were painted with iridescent paints reminding Hooker of the mother-of-pearl in the clear coats of lacquer on Mae. Mae looked nice and reflective but was dull compared to the enameling on the artifacts.

As they laid out the last pieces, the four stood back and just stared at the array filling the not so small table.

"Wow."

Chet nodded with pursed lips. "You can say that again, Squirt."

"What do you think it's all worth?" Hooker mumbled.

Micha shook his head. "How's your math. It's about fourteen and a half troy ounces to a pound, and the going rate for placer gold last summer was about one-fifty an ounce."

Hooker hiccupped a chuckle and looked at the Squirt. The kid moved his mouth then looked up. "Two thousand one hundred seventy-five per pound." Hooker smiled and gently slugged the kid's shoulder in slow motion as he looked back at Micha.

Micha looked past Hooker at the kid. "How the hell do you do that?"

The kid blushed, but Hooker explained. "He saw a multiplication table once. He just pulls it back up and looks for the right answer."

Micha scoffed at Hooker and looked at the kid. The Squirt rolled his lips in tight against his teeth and nodded as he rolled his shoulders in a moving shrug. "Pretty much. With numbers, they just seem to stack up and then just fall into the right order. But I can't really explain it, so Hooker's answer makes as much sense."

With the new information, they looked back at the

table. They all knew there was well over a hundred pounds on the table. Chet's eyes rolled into his head. "Just by the gold, it's a lot more than my house is worth."

Micha harrumphed. "A lot more than all of our houses... even Manny and Stella's house included."

"But for the historical value?" Hooker looked at the kid. "It's only something a museum should have." He turned to Chet for an answer.

The Highway Patrol Captain raised his hands. "Hey, you're the lead on this adventure. I'm just along for the good food."

Hooker glanced at his watch. "Crap. We have fifty-eight minutes to get to Dolly's for dinner."

The other three repacked the dive bags as Hooker scrambled up the hill to the truck. Opening the door and letting Box out to do his business, he grabbed the mic on the only radio always live—the straight line to Dolly.

"1-4-1," he called. He knew she was cooking and waited.

Dina, one of Dolly's night dispatchers, responded. "Go ahead, Hooker. Dolly is in the middle of the sauce."

"10-4, Dina. All four of us are out on the Snake and a little filthy..."

"Your mind has always been that way, Hooker." She was purring now. "So what's the problem?"

Hooker had to think about what the problem could be. Dolly knew Hooker had been with Chet and Micha all day, and they, along with the Squirt, would be his guests for the Wednesday night dinner. But she didn't know about why they were together or why Hooker was taking a few days off.

"This tow is a little more complicated than we initially thought." Hooker released the red button and hung his head. It was now dark, and he could see the glow of the South Bay Area filling the night air with light. This was one of the perks of his huge territory, which the other drivers who ran the close area of the city never saw. All they saw were the lighted streets where Hooker saw the beauty in the night sky.

Dolly's smooth, but out of breath voice came over the truck's speakers. "How many times have you sat at my table and were already filthy from an early tow?"

He knew there were too many to remember. "Ok, but we'll still be late."

"So is the other guest."

Hooker frowned. Dolly's table usually sat twelve. Who sat at the table on any given Wednesday night was up to Dolly, and they were hand-picked. Anyone who had ever sat at her table knew there was a reason they were there and on that night with those other guests. Not every evening's agenda was evident. But if you were sitting there, you were on Dolly's agenda. More promotions, contracts, or elections were won or lost at Dolly's table. It was why anyone in the know, knew the greater San Jose area was owned and run by Dolly. She knew everyone's secrets and where all of the skeletons were buried—a fact that at the moment was not lost on Hooker.

"Guest... as in singular?"

"Correct."

"We will be there as soon as we can, mama."

"Dinner will only be ready when you four are here. Oh, and Hooker... did you find who you were looking for?"

Hooker looked at the large ravine. In the dark, it was just a large winding tear of blacker black than the rest of the landscape. He slowly keyed the mic, thought a moment, and then gave her the answer. "Yes... yes, we did."

His lips rolled in as he thought about Maddie, and the special 'aunt' she had become to him of the last decade. The slight librarian who looked bow-legged and fragile had surprised Hooker time and again with her knowledge, her steel, and her resilient, tough nature and body. At sixty, she still rode an old Indian motorcycle she had ridden years before across the Bonneville Salt Flats at over two hundred miles an hour. The idea and act of which never ceased to amaze and amuse Hooker.

The voice of another strong woman in his life oozed protectively through the speaker. "You fellas drive careful. Dinner can wait. It's just food."

Hooker keyed the mic twice and hung it back up. Leaving the door open for Box, he scrambled back down the hill.

The table was empty, and Hooker could see Chet and Micha hiding the second body bag back under the brush and away from the streambed. "I guess we can just leave everything here?"

Chet stood with his hands on the small of his back stretching. The gray-haired flattop only came with age and creaky bones. "I think these will be good, but maybe the dive bags should come up, and you can stash them at Willie's until we figure out what to do with the stuff."

Micha nodded as he beat his work gloves on his overalls.

The Squirt patted Hooker on the shoulder as he walked past. "I'll send the line down with the cluster bags."

Hooker frowned after him. *What the hell are cluster bags?* His answer came minutes later.

When the wreck is so bad larger pieces become blasted off a car, Hooker had a couple of net bags he had picked up years before. The netting was made from a thin, soft bronze and lead cable that was very flexible but didn't break. Hanging from the J-hook were both bags. Hooker had never really called them anything—but you never need to name anything when you are the only person working. Hooker reflected a warm smile as he unhooked the newly named cluster bags. It was good to have the Squirt around.

Ten minutes later, the giant yellow truck followed Micha's cruiser as they wound their way down the Snake toward dinner. The three men in the truck were quiet, each lost in their own thoughts.

CHAPTER TEN

A S EACH OF THE men stepped through the large steel-plated door, they gently bent over and kissed the large woman, in the muumuu and bare feet, on the cheek. Nobody made it past Dolly without the appropriate greeting. Hooker was the last through the door as he stopped to pick up Box. Snuggling his nose and lips into her fat neck, he laid the twenty-plus pounds of scarred up orange tabby across her chest. The purring was instant. Box was in his heaven spot.

Dolly fussed like a little girl. "Hooker, damn it all, stop. You're a sick young man." As he started to pull away, her hand clamped on his neck and back of his head. "I didn't say right away." They both got the giggles, and Box mewed his discontent at their horseplay.

The man sitting in a chair by Dolly's desk, Chet had only seen once or twice before. There was not much reason for a Highway Patrol Officer to ever go up to the State

Supreme Court. He had seen Chief Justice Hitchcock 'The Knife' Hack when he had to sit in on court cases for classes.

The gentleman put down his cup of tea on Dolly's desk and rose quietly as the boisterous four horsemen bubbled out of the entry hall into the main dispatch room. He dabbed at his mouth with his handkerchief and slipped it in his slacks' pocket. The pencil-line mustache was a white line across his golf-tanned face.

Chet stepped over to make introductions. "Justice Hack, I'm—"

The man smiled perfunctorily and cut him off. "Please. Tonight I'm just Hitch. I believe you would be Chet, and this man would be Michael?"

"Micha, sir, short for Malachite, the stone, not the book in the bible."

The Justice smiled. "Yes, of course. I should have remembered from when I shook your hand at the academy graduation. You told me the same exact thing at the time, as well." Turning to Hooker, "Good to see you again, Hooker, and this must be the young man everyone is talking about." Hooker was trying to place the face.

John smiled and shortcutted the judge. "John, sir, but everyone calls me the Squirt."

"Yes," the judge nodded and shook his hand, "I had heard it happened. Well, let's see if we can get you through the academy quickly and on the road back to your own name, shall we?"

He looked at the mud stains on the bottoms of the jeans and caked in the nooks and crevices of their boots and shoes. "From the looks of things, you four had a productive day." Turning to face Hooker, "Are you finished, or is there more to do?"

Hooker thought about what this man might know and what he was willing to reveal at this time. After all, as Chet had alluded, this was in the gray area of clandestine. "I think there may be more to do, sir."

"Excuse me, gentlemen." Dolly stood in the door to the large kitchen with the long dining table. "You all know where the bathroom is to wash up. Dinner will be ready in ten minutes."

The dinner had been simple and adaptive—spaghetti with Dolly's special marinara sauce with Sicilian sausages from Chiaramonte's on North 13th Street. Tiny smears of the sauce were barely visible on the five plates where the garlic bread had all but hid the evidence.

In the other room, Hooker could hear the two dispatchers taking calls between bites. When Dolly cooks, everyone within reach eats. It was one of the perks or downfalls of the occupation. For eight hours, there was nothing to do but sit, take calls, and eat. The occupational hazard was evident in Dolly's quarter-ton and Dina's rapidly approaching the two hundred mark—pregnant or not. Karen, with over ten years working for Dolly, was somewhere in between. For Hooker, all of them had one thing in common—he loved nuzzling fat necks. It made them laugh, and they loved the attention, and it warmed Hooker's heart. He wasn't sure if it was love, but he did most certainly care deeply about his extended family. With Dolly and Stella, it was flat out unmitigated love.

Dolly put a large carafe of coffee in the middle of the

men clustered at one end of the table. "Gentlemen, there is no dessert tonight. If you need anything sweet, we three girls will be just outside this door." Uncharacteristically, she closed the door.

Since the start of Hooker's obligatory attendance of her Wednesday night dinner and been placed as the anointed head of the table, he had never seen her leave the room or close the door. Never.

He turned toward the judge. Up until now, the conversations had been light and covered sports or amusing little things going on in the South Bay, like shootings and which Mafia was moving into what area, and would Stanford football ever be anything other than a joke. The judge felt Hooker's scrutiny.

"You have a question, Hooker, and I'm guessing it is about my being here."

Hooker nodded. "Outside of us, there are maybe only three other people who even knew what we were doing today."

The judge looked down at his mug of cooling coffee. He thought about trust and knowledge and the power of those, as well as how fragile they could be. He looked up at Hooker. "You don't know anything about me, other than those times I stopped by the hospital after Manny had been shot. My family, well, my sister still owns about two thousand acres of truck farm down in the Hollister area. When I was a kid, we had about double the spread over near Salinas. There was a road running down the middle of our spread. Because it ran in and around homesteads, it had many very tight turns at the corners of the property.

The moonshine runners used to call it El Camino d' El Diablo, The Devil's Highway. That road was the collecting road..."

Hooker finished "The south end of the Snake."

The judge nodded. "Parked outside is my Lincoln Town Car. Parked in my garage is a 1968 Road Runner with a 1970 440 six-pack Super Commander with a custom-built Max Wedge clip and shaker hood. William and Maddie balanced the four-speed with a 4:11 rear end. William tubbed the rear and clipped the axle for an extra four inches on each side. On a piss poor night up at Fremont, I can blow the doors on some low eights. If I want the mid-sevens, I will have to insert a roller and chute. Then it would just be a factor of adjusting for the alcohol." He blinked as he watched Hooker take it all in.

"What color?"

"B-5 blue."

Hooker blinked but maintained eye contact. "The torque ripped a hole on the left side, so we welded in an eight by twelve of quarter-inch plate. The torsion bars Stimson Moly steel from Sweden, they took four months to make and get here. The pressure in the clutch is twelve pounds off a hair-trigger, and your back seat is a bucket hold for gallon bottles."

The two had just gone behind the barn and pissed as high up the wall as they could. They had compared penises, sniffed each other's butts, and come away satisfied. The judge was a silent member of the family.

Hooker looked at the other three and nodded. The tension waned as Chet reached for the coffee carafe and held it up. "More coffee... Hitch?" The man smiled and pushed out his mug.

Hooker looked at his mug and asked, "How much do you know?"

The judge sipped his hot coffee and thought. Placing his mug on the table, he frowned slightly. "Two days ago, I caught wind of a potential territorial dispute involving a found skeleton. In these kinds of matters, they usually make their way up to us in San Francisco, so it's not unusual for us to get some kind of early warning.

"Then, all of a sudden, there is no dispute. In fact, there is nothing. It was as if no skeleton had been found. That's when our antennas really go up and start to vibrate so hard the tips start hitting the walls in the hallways. Because when there is a case and then a case disappears, one of two things has happened. Either the FBI rolled into town, or the case just went underground.

"We didn't see or hear of any Feds swinging their dicks down this way, so we knew it was going dark. That, gentleman, is a very worrisome occurrence because it usually ends up with the need to fill some vacancies in the department. But then, last night I got a call from an old friend. He told me he had a hand and a watch. He also thought it would be in the interest of many to make a dinner reservation at the most powerful restaurant in the Bay Area.

"I kind of remember Danny, but he was a little older than me. I went to school with his kid sister. When I called down this morning to leave a message, Dolly was already here. She confirmed you four were out digging around. So I figured I'd come down to find out what was going on and to assure you four I have your back. From here on out, you are investigating an old case I have full knowledge of, and it is being kept under wraps and within my purview.

"Legally, as of this afternoon, you four are attached to my office and are investigating a case that may or may not exceed the boundaries of the local authority. So with all that and the powers vested in me and my office, I hereby deputize the four of you as bench investigators, and you only answer to me in these matters until we reach an agreement or resolve the case to meet with jurisprudence. Do I have your agreements?"

Micha was quick. "Does this mean I don't have to burn days off?"

Hitch smiled. "Working for me pays a lot more than you make on the street. And it also means more than just the paycheck. You are all on my office payroll for the duration. Including the Squirt..." he glared at Hooker, "especially the Squirt."

The four looked stunned at the turn of events and nodded.

The judge raised his mug to his lips and looked at Hooker. "So, where are we?"

Hooker raised his eyebrows at the other conspirators and leaned back to fish the keys out of his pocket. Throwing them across. The Squirt's hand was already in the air, "You only need to bring in one."

The Squirt rose and left, reclosing the door.

Hooker turned to the judge. "We've excavated two whole skeletons so far. The Squirt thinks he could feel at least two more. He also thinks that will be it unless there are more under those two. The cavity stops in the back with a large boulder, so we know it doesn't go back any farther. The overhead is pretty solid as well.

"There is a hulk of a late 1930 or early 1940 four-door sedan down there. We're pretty sure it's connected. The back seat is the same as your Road Runner. It wasn't a serious shine-runner, but more of a gentleman's runner. So we're sure it was owned by someone who didn't need to run the Snake."

The judge mused. "What about the VIN numbers?"

Chet coughed. "Rusted out." He smirked at Hooker. "Hooker stuck his hand straight through the punch-out where the plate should have been."

Micha added, "And the engine was a hot-rod out of a Lincoln straight-eight."

"So if the engine was stuffed in during the war years, then there probably would be no record of sale we could use to trace it either."

Hooker wagged his head as he scratched at the long scars on his head. "No, and nothing survived to identify the other body either. If it weren't for the watch being all high-quality metal, we wouldn't have anything."

The door opened, and the Squirt slipped in with one of the dive bags. Without saying a word, he handed it and the keys to Hooker. The judge's eyebrows raised as he watched Hooker's smirk pull to one side.

Hooker stood. "There is one tiny complication to all of this..." As he up-ended the bag on the table in front of them, the gold objects flowed out. A large scarab skittered across the table and landed in the judge's lap.

Hooker sat as the judge raised the object from his lap. His eyes were huge as he looked at the unexpected sculpture. He knew what he held was well over a pound of pure gold. But the detail and craftsmanship of the sculpture went well beyond the mere value of the gold. The enameled blue iridescent wings rippled purple to red in the fluorescent light. On the belly were incised or carved ancient Egyptian hieroglyphics.

Micha sipped his coffee then commented. "We ran the math. You're holding about three grand of gold."

The judge looked up in horror. "But the value of the piece..."

He was looking at four slow nodding smirks.

"And this was in the cavity with the bones?"

Hooker nodded. "And three more bags just like this."

The judge picked up a small bowl and a chain. Looking closely, he ran his fingers over the engravings. "But these aren't just a small collection some collector would have. These are more like what you would find in a museum." He pushed his glasses up onto his head and brought the fine chain closer to his face. "A wealthy collector and I know a few in San Francisco who might have a couple of items like this along with some pottery shards..." he looked up and waved his palm at the hoard on the table, "but this alone would be a prized exhibit of any museum."

"That was our thinking," Chet said, looking over the rim of his coffee.

The Squirt mused, not sure of his position. "You mentioned you knew some collectors...?"

The judge looked up and drew down his glasses slowly.

"Yes, but not ones into Egyptology. My friends run more toward more recent and local in their predilections. West Coast Indian baskets or weaponry is more their speed. Certainly, not anyone who even starts down the road toward idols or ancient art craft of this quality," he held up the scarab, "and most certainly not in such precious metals."

As he carefully placed the scarab, bowl, and chain back with the other loot, he then looked around the table. "Any ideas where you plan to proceed from here?" His eyes rested on Hooker. The judge sensed that despite his youth, Hooker was the central figurehead of the group.

Hooker watched his finger smudge along the table. "There is a museum in Santa Clara..."

CHAPTER ELEVEN

WHEN HOOKER FINALLY pulled up out front, the museum was, in a way, what he expected —but not *where* he expected it. The last many blocks, Hooker kept frowning. The residential neighborhood was known as the Rose Garden District. With pristinely manicured lawns as display floors of specimen sized and tended shrubbery and trees, the last sort of building he expected was a large Egyptian temple with colored columns and an expanse of land.

Hooker eyed the large lawn. He swung open the door with his boot. "Go ahead, Box."

As the cat stood stiff-legged peeing on the lawn, Hooker quietly sat thinking. They had called ahead, and he had an appointment with the director of the museum, a man named James Sutter.

Box finished, scratched, and started looking around for any dogs he could tear up while he was in an easy pickings type of neighborhood. Hooker just closed his eyes and slowly shook his head. Hooker had found the large cat as a tiny kitten in a box abandoned under a stripped car behind the Almaden winery. The kitten had been badly beaten up as well as chewed up, obviously by a dog or dogs. Hooker had put the box with the kitten in his truck and hauled him to a vet. The kitten had purred the entire way and even as the vet examined him while Hooker held him. The vet had tried to convince Hooker the little life would be better off being put down. Hooker knew better, and the vet had spent hours patching him up. The cat and Hooker had been partners ever since.

"Come on, Box. There is nothing here for you to have a good fight. This kind of neighborhood is filled with nothing but bait like Poodles and Yorkies." A woman who was walking her Yorkie heard Hooker, and with horror in her eyes, scooped up her precious piece of fluff, turned around, and quickened her walk as she retreated. Hooker closed his eyes and pinched the bridge of his nose.

Box watched the retreating target with his one eye in critical evaluation, and then bound back into the truck to settle in his box. Hooker scratched Box's head and twiddled with his one ear. "I have an important meeting in here. So stay in the truck until I get back. Maybe we can get some ice cream after I get out."

He slid from the truck and closed the door with the window still open. He never believed in locking Box in. Box was his partner, and not a possession to be locked up.

As he entered the museum, he saw a small sign pointing toward the offices. The woman at a desk mulling over a document looked up surprised. "May I help you?"

Hooker had the feeling the museum didn't get a lot of foot traffic.

"My name is Hooker, and I have an appointment with a Mr. Sutter..." The woman was blinking as if she were trying to see if Hooker was real or just her imagination.

Suddenly, she came to a conclusion. "Oh, yes, you called earlier." She picked up the phone on her desk and dialed a few numbers. "Yes, James, the man is here to see you. A Mr. Hooker?"

She replaced the phone in the cradle and looked up at Hooker, blinking rapidly. "He'll be right down." She blinked some more and then returned to mulling over whatever she had been reading before.

Hooker watched her with silent and hidden amusement. A deadpan face while you should be laughing was a game he learned to play with Manny and Stella. Not reacting to conversations or events had held him in good stead many times during towing—from the hilariously stupid to the tragic insanity humanity visits upon itself at high and low speeds.

"Mr. Hooker, I presume?"

Hooker turned to take in a slight mouse of a man with a bowtie. "It's just Hooker, sir."

"No first name, or is that your first name?" They shook. His grip was interestingly firm and friendly.

"Actually, a combination of all of it. Horatio Octavio O'Keller; for most people, it is just easier to use Hooker."

The man blinked a few times. Hooker was sure he must be related to the woman. "Hooker it is then. How may I help you?"

Hooker thought about the woman and what he needed to ask. His antenna was up, and he could feel her attention was more in her ears than it was toward what she had been reading. "Maybe you could show me a little bit of the museum, and we can talk as we walk."

The man glanced at his watch. Hooker was sure it was more of an affectation to let Hooker know he was a busy man, more than his checking the time. "I won't take much of your valuable time."

The man considered the young man in a leather jacket, white t-shirt, and jeans over work boots. He was certain he would not be spending much time with whatever this young man of the street wanted. He nodded and held out his hand. "Then let us start with the main gallery, shall we?"

As they entered the impressive gallery with a diorama display of an ancient Egyptian city, the man started in a routine script. "The Rosicrucian Museum was originally founded by Dr. Harvey Spencer Lewis in the early days of the 1920s. He funded several archeological digs while augmented his original collection. The collection started with a small Sekhmet statue but soon grew. In 1928, Dr. Lewis presented to the public a collection he named The Rosicrucian Egyptian Oriental Museum. It was originally housed in what is now the administration building."

Hooker looked about the main gallery. "So this is not the original building?"

"Oh, no. The collection had grown over the years, and in the sixties, Dr. Lewis's son secured the funds to build this building, as well as the gardens."

"What about the smaller items? Like the statue or

jewelry? *Life* magazine did quite an issue on King Tut. There seemed to be a lot of gold artifacts."

The man blinked as he studied the young street tough dressed in a leather jacket. He wasn't sure about his safety at the moment.

Hooker sensed the man's unease. He slipped his right hand into his pants pocket and withdrew the large scarab. He held it out to the director. The man slowly took it and examined it carefully.

As the director turned the scarab over and saw the writing on the underside, Hooker spoke softly. "Let's talk about 1953."

The man looked up, almost dropping the artifact. His face was as shocked as if Hooker had just slapped him. Hooker knew he had just hit pay dirt.

"Come with me." The small man turned and walked into another gallery and stood in front of a case where there were two matching scarabs—duplicates of the one in the man's hand. The man looked to Hooker with a question on his face.

Hooker held his gaze for a few moments and then began examining each of the display cases in turn. There were a few pieces Hooker didn't recognize, but for the most part, this was the same collection he knew was in four dive bags.

He finally turned to face the man who was waiting patiently for him. He had the man's full attention as well as his curiosity. Hooker gracefully waved his palm around the gallery. "All or at least most of these are fakes."

The man stood for a moment and then silently nodded.

He held up the scarab in his hand. There was a question on his face. Hooker nodded. "By the weight, you can tell it is not a fake."

The man sagged as his hand dropped to his side. He then stepped over to Hooker and handed him the scarab back. "Maybe we should go to the administration office to have this conversation."

As they walked across the grounds, which was an Egyptian garden King Tutankhamen would have felt at home in, the man started to ask Hooker a question, then stopped. He looked about at the deserted gardens. Finally, he stopped. "You have to see this from my perspective. From out of the blue, a young man who looks like he rides a motorcycle with a gang brings me a sacred statue and then tells me all of our other treasures are fakes..."

Hooker empathized with the man. "Trust me for a little while longer. I mean no harm. I'm just looking to make something right again."

"But how did you come by..."

"For now, let's just leave it at... I found it." Hooker examined the man's pained eyes.

The man turned, and they continued toward the distant building.

As they entered the man's office, he offered a seat with his hand. "Can I get you something to drink?"

"No, I'm fine, thank you."

James picked up the phone and dialed a local number. Hooker could hear the rings on the other end. Someone picked up. "Hello, Donald, it's James over at the museum. I have a gentleman in my office who I believe you need to talk to. Could you come over, please?"

Hooker heard the sound of the response. The man thanked him and hung up.

He leaned back in his chair, looking at Hooker. Hooker was certain he was a great mystery to this man. "Donald won't be long. He only lives a block from here." His right hand waved behind him. He leaned forward to the desk. "Could I see it again... please?"

Hooker fished the scarab out of his pocket and passed it across. The man sat looking at the inscription on the underside. Hooker could tell he knew what it said and was in his own world at the moment. Hooker watched as the man became less and less attached to the room they were in. It was the kind of concentration he was familiar with watching Manny with a case or Willie with an engine or another complicated auto part. He even saw it in Maddie, as she would pour over a book containing information she wanted. It was the focus of a person who knew so much about what they were looking at it was as if it were a part of their identity.

A light rap on the doorframe startled Hooker. The elder gentleman in chinos and a sweater looked in. "Hello, you're the gentleman I am to talk to?"

James looked up and blinked several times, orienting himself. He squinted. "Oh, yes, Donald." He stood with his hand out toward Hooker, who was also rising.

Hooker stuck his hand out. "My name is Hooker."

"Pleased to meet you, Donald Phelps."

James made the connection. "Donald was the director in 1953."

The elder man's head whipped around to look at James,

and then he noticed the scarab in his hand. Looking back at Hooker, there was a new light in his eye. Hooker knew the look. It was one that usually appeared in the eye of an animal who knew it was prey.

Hooker softened his demeanor. "I come in peace." They both looked at James, who was standing pinching the bridge of his nose as he held the scarab out for Donald to take.

The man took the object and gave it a cursory exam. James cinched the suspicion. "He knows. All of it."

The older man took the only other chair in the room. He collapsed. Hooker watched as the man deflated, and then became at rest as if a great weight had been lifted. He held up the scarab and looked at Hooker. "So this...?"

"Is the real one." Hooker nodded.

The man rolled his lips tight against his teeth. "So what now?"

Hooker sat as he watched James do the same. "What happens now... is you tell me what happened in 1953."

"1953..." the man's eyes became unfocused, and his head drifted off course and came to rest, looking out the second-story window, "what happened... should have never happened. I had only been recently elected to the position of director then. There were only a few paid positions in those days. A lot of the work was done by members of the society. We were basically a volunteer organization back then."

"Society?"

"The Ancient Mystical Order Roseae Crucis." He said it as if Hooker would or should have knowledge of it, so

Hooker didn't ask for clarification. The education could come later at the hands of Maddie. Hooker just nodded.

"The guard duties were rotated through the membership. Mostly, it was a boring routine of wandering about the museum. Especially, the night duty—a tour of boring torture, from usually about eight at night until six in the morning when the cleaning volunteers would come to prepare the museum for guests. Even when it was in this building, the sweeping and dusting was a long and labor-intensive job for the four volunteers." Hooker could read the suffering on the man's face. Obviously, he had been a longtime volunteer before landing the job of director.

The man, laying his head back, remembered the pain or headache of the night in question. "We had a young man who was an almost regular volunteer for the night duty. We later learned he used the nights to either catch up on his rest or engage in unseemly activities with his fiancée."

He leaned his head forward to see if Hooker understood the circumstances. Hooker did.

"Well, obviously, those night forays into their indiscretions had a result, and they needed to get married. And in those days, the only place you could get married, in the middle of the night, in the Bay Area was in the Tenderloin of San Francisco. As to whether the bond was legitimate or not has no bearing on this matter. Suffice it to say, one night, this guard took the liberty of being unsupervised and ran off with his girl to elope. When he returned, about four in the morning, the one gallery had been sacked.

"There was a member who did private investigations, but there was no evidence of entry at the time. He snooped about but could never turn up any leads. It was as if the items had literally vanished in a puff of smoke."

He smiled as he leaned forward. "I can tell you... it was the spookiest thing ever. Some of the marginal members, who were only interested as a cursory association, fled. Others, seeing it as one of the great mysteries, became staunch. It had a very galvanizing effect on the select membership, who was in the know of inner workings—such as the board."

He lay back. "Years later, we had some major work done on the roof, and one of the workers discovered the pins in the hinges to one of the trap doors had been removed and then put back, thus using the lock as the hinge. The doors are large and heavily insulated with rock wool bats. The only key to the lock is kept in this office, and the lock is unique. Nobody ever suspected the weak link, as it were, was the hinge."

"Why didn't you call the police?"

"The last thing we wanted was a scandal and for the word to get out that the most valuable items in the museum had flown the coop. The membership would have had our hides for book covers and then fled with their money. You see, the membership provides and supports the museum, not the other way around."

"So you made the fakes."

He nodded. "It was the only course we could think of at the time. We closed the gallery for renovations and kept stalling the general membership about this problem until we had obtained the faux artifacts. Once we reopened the gallery, the only hard part was keeping the secret safe between these walls." He held his hands out to indicate the walls of the office.

"So the secret of 1953 was passed down from director to director." The former director nodded a mirror of the current one. Hooker pursed his lips, thinking, and then frowned. "So where do you go to get fakes made without the membership catching wind of it?"

The older man smiled, rubbed at his nose, and then tossed his hand in dismissal. "To the source, of course. We went back to Egypt with a stack of photographs. Several of the artifacts were already being knocked off by very good artisans, like the scarab, for instance. The iridescent enameling on the gold is a secret formula handed down for millennia within families of artisans there in Egypt. So we could simply look for the best representatives and purchase them as tourist trinkets."

Hooker smiled softly. "And simply re-establish the exhibit and voila, nobody is the wiser."

The man nodded. "Along with a few new flourishes to justify the long delay and renovations to the exhibit. In those days, fresh paint was enough, but when you throw in a few new artifacts, there is renewed excitement instead of suspicion or resentment."

Hooker knew he was missing something. "So did anyone ever figure out who actually did the theft?"

"Not conclusively. We had our suspicions, but we had no way to prove anything. We might have found fingerprints, but without going to the police, they wouldn't do us any good. So we never pursued any more investigations. We simply installed the fakes and carried on with our lives as if nothing had ever happened. Until today..."

"Who did you suspect?" Hooker asked.

"About time, we were having a lot of work done. There was a new roof being laid and then installation of a modern air conditioning system. With all of that, there were electricians, roofers, sheet metal men, plumbers... and the list goes on. Any one of the workers or group of workers could have done it."

Hooker thought about the different workers. "Would you still have the work orders or receipts?"

The older director looked to the newer. James frowned as he pursed his lips. "I suppose... maybe down in storage." He turned to Hooker. "Why? What good would it do? It was twenty years ago. Some or most of those companies are probably out of business by now."

"Maybe, but I have a hunch it may help me figure this all out." He glanced at his watch and stood. "I have to be somewhere else now, but if you could see about finding those records, I can see about finding more of what was stolen from you." He fished out his wallet and removed a business card. "When you find something, you can always reach me through this number." He placed the card on the desk.

The older director looked once again at the scarab then offered it to Hooker.

Hooker held up his hand in a stop. "No, keep it. It is rightfully yours. Let's call it a down payment in good faith."

The two men smiled and nodded, and then handed it

back to Hooker. "We know he will come back to us... after he has gathered his friends."

Hooker knew if the receipts still existed, they would find them. After all, a museum is all about artifacts and record-keeping.

CHAPTER TWELVE

H OOKER SCRAMBLED DOWN the hillside into the ravine. The other three were under the canopy arranging bones in a body bag. Hooker noticed one more bag off to the side. He glanced over at the hole in the hillside. There seemed to be a flat, scraped-smooth floor. Even the pickiest of bears would find it in move-in condition.

"Four total?"

Chet looked up. "According to our expert excavator here, yes, it would appear so."

The Squirt looked up the ravine and wiped at his face. Turning, he looked at Hooker. His eyes were red and wet. He passed the tip of his tongue along his drawn lips. "I know I don't want to do forensics or crime scene stuff." He nodded back at the cavern. "All of the walls are firm and weren't dug at. The same holds true for the bottom." He reached in his front left pocket. "Here, I also found these this morning." He laid a pair of dog tags and what was left of the chain in Hooker's hand.

Hooker looked at the name. They were Danny's tags.

Micha cleared his throat as he began to zip up the bag. "We figure he didn't stop off when he hit the base. Probably landed in San Francisco and took a bus or something down to Ord. Somewhere along the way, he got off."

"That would explain why the family never saw him come home." Micha and Chet nodded.

Chet bent down and picked up a piece of rusted rippled metal. Anyone who drove in the United States could tell you what it was just by the shape. "The Squirt here figured out the license number. I called it in. It took a while, but they found the records in Sacramento. It was registered to a 1926 Diamond T truck."

Hooker kicked at the dirt. "Crap."

Chet chuckled. "Not so fast, and you owe the jar a few dollars by my count."

Hooker smiled up at the man. He knew Chet was right. He had been kind of gutter-mouthed lately.

Chet bent down again and came up with some old papers. "This is your employee's responsibility here."

The Squirt smiled but blushed. Shyly, he turned toward Hooker. "I got to thinking about how people are lazy. There are a lot of people who never put their front license plate on the front. So I figured most people would just put it where it would be convenient."

Hooker slapped his forehead with the heel of his hand. "The trunk."

Chet smiled. "It was still wrapped in the oil-paper they

used to send them out wrapped in. The oil and wax and the fact it was above most of the flooding saved it from rusting out." He pulled the license out of the paper. The black letters still shined as did most of the yellow background.

Hooker smiled at the plate and then looked up at Chet, and then the Squirt. "Damn, kid, I might even have to start paying you a wage."

"You mean more than the two roofs over my head, food to make me fat, and all the grief you can heap on me? Oh, Massa, Squirt don't deserve such goodness." In horror, he looked over at Micha. "I didn't mean anything, Micha."

The man was looking at the kid pensively. He reached out his hand and rested it on the Squirt's shoulder. "I know you didn't. I was just thinking about how good it sounded. I wonder if I can get away with something similar with my wife."

None of them were laughing. But they did see the humor. Hooker cautioned, "We've met your wife, Micha. I don't think you had better even try it with Bobbie Sue. I don't know which I would be afraid of most, the Injun side or the Cajon."

Micha looked at Hooker with big eyes and a smirk. "Good point, Hooker. I think I'll just stick with the successful 'Yes, Dear.'"

Hooker smiled and looked at Chet. "So did you run this plate, too?"

"Was wondering when we were getting back to the serious work at hand." He looked at the plate in his hand. "As a matter of fact, it came back to a 1937 Chevrolet Master Deluxe." He turned to look at the rusted hulk. "I would say it fits the bill. Heavy suspension, oversized brakes, and plenty of room for an extra tank or a hold box like this one. Four doors and by the end of the war, they were on used lots for two or three ten-spots. People were very tired of driving the same old car for ten or twelve years. The bulletproof rear-ends were great for making into hill climbers, too. So, if you wanted an unassuming car that would never get a second glance, and could run some great amount of moonshine, this would be your car."

"And it was registered to..."

"A Giovinito something. I think it's a Greek name. I've got it written down up at the car and the address, too." He leaned on the table with a flat hand. "No matter what, it's not going to be a very hot lead. The guy died in 1961. The car was last registered in 1952. So it's still an uphill battle."

Hooker looked at the very tired man. "If solving mysteries was easy, everyone would do it." Neither blinked nor smiled. Although it was true, it still made Hooker an outlier. But Hooker would be the first to admit—it wasn't just him—it was his family.

Hooker stood with Micha at the bottom of the ravine as they watched the last of the equipment being winched up by the Squirt. The afternoon had turned chilly, and the two were back in their jackets with four hands stuffed in pockets.

Micha waxed into common memories. "Who would have thought, all those years ago, standing in the rain with a prom queen dead in your arms, we would be digging up four skeletons and a mystery?"

Hooker thought about the defining night in their friendship as he watched the large package of tent and table slowly ascended the cliff. The chill of the evening underscored the memory.

It had been a large wreck with many cars creatively parking all over the south and northbound lanes of the 101 freeway. The last of the cars had been towed by various other wreckers when the then fifteen-year-old Hooker, driving on a bogus license, noticed a red truck parked wrong in the garden area of the cloverleaf of the two crossing freeways.

Hooker pointed out the truck in the dark and rain to Micha. They ran across the southbound lanes from the wide median. Hooker saw a young girl sitting in the driver's side. He asked if she was all right through the door. As he opened the door, she slumped over into his arms, asking him to please not let her die. She was gone by the time Micha came up behind Hooker a couple of heartbeats later. The two young men stood in the rain, letting it wash away their anguish.

Hooker watched as the Squirt reeled in the extended boom, and the package disappeared over the cliff edge. Thinking of Maddie and finding her brother Danny after all these years, he turned to the Highway Patrol Officer and friend. "Who knew a dying prom queen would be the easy one?"

With fists stuffed in their jackets, the two men strolled down the ravine to what had become the easiest access to the road above. Hooker could feel the weight of the season bearing down. It would become busier for towing as the drunks worked hard at filling his nights. People would force the smiles and joyousness into their voices with each new holiday—to suppress the disappointments, or loneliness became all too obvious. Also, would be the holes in lives—from people no longer there.

Hooker clinched the dog tags that had become hot in his pocket. And as he began to climb the hill, he thought with apprehension about the talk he would soon have to have with Maddie.

CHAPTER THIRTEEN

"Hooker?" Hooker grabbed the mic from behind his head. "Go ahead, Dispatch."

Karen, the day manager's voice eased across from the speaker. "I know you vampires hate being out at this hour, but there is a tow you may have some interest in. Fly is on the line and wants an answer, toot sweet."

Hooker dropped two gears and pulled the large Bakelite steering wheel into the slow cloverleaf onto 680 headed north. He glanced over at the Squirt and the side mirror to watch the mangled bread truck wobble behind. Straightening out onto the freeway, he merged and clicked through the lost two gears, adding another.

Keying the red button, "What's the Fly got in her web?"

There was a moment's silence as Hooker signaled left and changed lanes as he overtook an empty produce-hauling trailer and tractor. The season was gone, so the wire mesh trailers were hauled north to Oregon to be filled with the Christmas trees the Bay Area consumed.

The radio sparked. "Seventy-two Mack, max twin, long boy with a nose who lost the fight with the 247 Express last night." Hooker followed the shorthand of towing large trucks. The newer Mack truck was probably a long-haul or over the road, with a driving team who didn't know where they were and had stopped on the railroad tracks to look at a map. It wasn't the first time he had seen this kind of fatal mistake, but rarely was it made by drivers with enough experience to drive overweight loads.

"What was the load?"

"Forty-two-foot Grand Banks fishing boat."

"Do I get the trailer, too?" Hooker smiled over at the Squirt and wiggled his eyebrows. "You think your sister would like to go out fishing with me?" The Squirt laughed.

"She says the boat is toast, but you get the double haul with the empty sled."

Hooker eased off the fuel as he signaled to exit. Dropping a gear, he flipped the switch on the Jake break— flooding air into the engine to create backpressure, gently slowing the rig. As he flicked off the Jake and its hammering noise—illegal on city streets, he keyed the mic.

"Where's it at, and how soon does she want it?"

"She needs the tractor before Monday morning and the trailer anytime by Wednesday."

"What's the catch?" Three days to tow a truck was too easy.

"It's in the Salinas Impound."

Hooker smiled. "Is it cleared?"

"Insurance has written off on it, so it's good to tow."

Just when he needed to go snoop in the area, it didn't

get better than that. Hooker smiled. "Tell her I'll drop by later for the papers. She'll have both of them in the back lot by Sunday night."

"10-4, Hooker. Dispatch out."

Hooker double-clicked the key as he hung the mic behind his head. Thinking, he dropped four gears and wagged the gear shifter in neutral as he rolled to a stop at a red light.

"So it looks like we get paid to go track down this Giovanni guy?" The Squirt smiled out the passenger window over his leather-jacketed arm, mirroring Hooker. An early Christmas gift from their friend Sweets and his brother Danny was greatly appreciated by both the Squirt and Hooker. The uniform of the day in the truck was a black leather jacket over starched white t-shirt, jeans, and boots unless your natural uniform was orange and white striped fur.

"It would seem so." Hooker's smirk pulled to the right and away from the still fresh scars. His right hand dangled and found the single fuzzy ear. His stomach growled as he thought about lunch on the piers of Monterey's Cannery Row—*and maybe we can find Box a little fresh crab or fish for lunch, too.*

Minutes later, they stood at the back end of Mae. "Sounds like a sweet deal. We get to jerk a prom queen and a Betty to pay the fuel, and it puts us down where we need to be—to seriously do some detective work, too." The Squirt ran the levers to drop the bread truck while Hooker finished the paperwork.

"Ever have crab so fresh you choose it out of a tank,

watch it boil, and then sit on the end of a wharf and eat it out of a pile of newspaper?"

The Squirt looked over as he let go of the levers. "I've never had crab before. Does it taste like shrimp? Because I've had shrimp at the diner a few times, and it was good." He went to unhook the J-hooks from the front axle of the bread truck.

Hooker watched him in horror. "You're not talking about those little things with all the breading they deep fry, are you?"

The Squirt stood up, and his eyebrows flared up, and then he frowned. "Yeah, why?"

Hooker slowly closed his eyes as his face fell forward to meet his hand as he muttered, "Oh, Saint Dolly and Willie, save me from the children." He looked up at the sound of approaching footsteps.

"They told me you were fast, but I didn't expect you until after midnight." The pudgy, balding office type strolled up with a check in his hand. He stuck out his right hand. "Joss Baker."

"Hooker. Someone broke into the crypt, and when we found out we didn't burn up in the sunlight, we figured we might as well just do some towing."

The man chuckled, and they exchanged check and bill. Hooker pointed at the large dent-gash in the side. "She was tracking with a wobble. I think you are probably looking at a bent frame."

"So it's not repairable?"

"You need to talk to your insurance adjuster. If it's worth enough, then I'll probably be back out to pull it down to the Fly in San Jose or over to Alex's over in San Leandro. Both can take it off the frame and re-rack the frame straight. It's what they do every day." Hooker handed the man his business card, as well as the Fly's.

"We'll let you know." The man tapped the cards on his thumb holding the paperwork. "Thanks for the quick response."

The Squirt walked up, slapping his gloves in his open hand. "We're here whenever you need a quickie." The man frowned until the kid pointed out the slogan painted on the side of the towing boom: *Southside Hooker — When you need a quickie.*

The man smiled and waved as he walked away.

Hooker smiled at the Squirt.

"What?"

Hooker laughed and shook his head. "Nothing." He leaned his weight back on his heels and looked down his nose at the kid. "So, boss, where to now?"

The kid glanced at his watch. Then his face brightened. "Time for a little massage therapy."

Hooker's face pulled to the one side as he nodded in a smirk. *You learn fast, kid.*

CHAPTER FOURTEEN

THE LIGHT LUNCH after their massages had also been a stalling tactic. Hank liked having Candy, and whoever the other student was, around. But Willie had called Maddie to see if she could get away from the library for a while for a long lunch.

Candy and the other student had been properly hugged and sent on their way back to school. The dishes were cleared, and only the coffee mugs and carafe cluttered the table. The room was quiet, as Hank had decided he needed to run into town to get something to fix for dinner. Willie sat next to the woman, who had been his best friend for as long as he cared to remember, quietly holding her hand.

Hooker watched the woman stare at the watch and dog tags he had just placed on the table in front of her. He studied the small twitch in the jaw muscle that was there when she was figuring out things. Usually, it was about ratios in engines or rear-ends of cars to make them faster or better. This time, it was more about a weight that had been in her heart for a long time.

In the soft light coming through the north-facing window over the sink, Hooker studied the gray hairs. They had snuck in so slowly over the course of their friendship Hooker had forgotten how old she truly was. She had been about fifty when he had met her ten years before.

After taking Hooker in, Willie had told the kid he wasn't going to make him go to school knowing he would just run away again. But he did insist his education be continued. Nobody had mentioned it would also continue even after Hooker had passed his GED. Now, at twenty-five, he was still held to reading, learning, and papers or reports on as wide a range of subjects as there were aisles in the library she ran.

Hooker thought back to the first day she had sat down at the reading desk. Hooker had no idea who this slight bandy-legged older woman was. Her hair was pulled back in a hard tight bun. Hooker for years figured she had to use a come-a-long to pull it so tight until he made a smart-assed remark, and her small hand descended onto and then into his shoulder. The pain wouldn't have been as great if he had simply placed his shoulder in a bench vice and run it home until the collar-bone cracked. The small steely grip carried a lesson he never forgot. Smartass remarks were only made in jest and should never carry even a hint of malice or hurt.

Hooker harrumphed with a soft, silent chuckle. How was he to know back then he would eventually have a large extended family who held a daily interrelationship Olympics in smartass remarks? Never in malice. All jabs carried an unspoken but understood message of love, trust, and ultimate caring. As Willie had become his trusted, much-loved uncle, Maddie was his aunt.

From the first day, Hooker had learned this woman who looked frail in her demeanor and walk, slow to speak and sparse in her movements was, in fact, considered to be one of the fastest women in cars or on motorcycles. The large Indian Chief motorcycle she occasionally rode was the same one she set the land speed record at the Bonneville Salt Flats. She was the first woman to ride a motorcycle over 200 mph. Her second required pass had resulted in her having to step off the motorcycle at over 150 mph. It took two years to repair her and the motorcycle and return to lock in the title. It wasn't the first of her major accidents, nor would it be the last.

The last, she had shared with Willie in a 1963 Dodge Dart GT with a 340 Hemi engine. The resulting many loops and rolls were the result of too much wine, too late at night, too long of a day, and a slightly damp highway where a few deer stood in the headlights.

Every day, Hooker was thankful the two old birds were too tough to kill.

But now he was watching her have to deal with something she couldn't outrun or out think. Her past was rushing out to smack her as sure as an oncoming freight train.

Her free hand shook as it slowly reached out and almost touched the watch. Then it retreated to her cover her mouth. There were no tears. But her spare frame trembled with emotion that had nowhere to go. She stared at the watch and then leaned over to Willie's shoulder. Her head rested on the soft pillow at the top of his arm. Her voice was thin and distant. "We took the train up to San Francisco. I wore the canary yellow dress you like so much. You said it reminded you of the mustard blossoms in the springtime back when the hills behind Watsonville were farmed by the Japanese."

Willie squeezed her hand. "I liked the dress because it made you look like a woman. And when your father saw you dressed in it, he knew he hadn't ruined you with all the greasy iron racing and running shine. It made him happy, and I think it made him also think of your mama."

She glanced up at him with only a hint of surprise. She then snuggled her head back onto his shoulder as she started to reach for the watch again. Her hand hovered there in the air and then withdrew to rest on her heart. "We had supper while they engraved the back. To my Golden Knight, with love from your little sister..."

She drew in a fluttering breath through her half-open mouth, held it, and then slowly let out so much long endured pain.

She looked over at the silent Squirt, and then to Hooker. "How?"

Hooker sighed. "We don't know yet. There were four bodies altogether. Only this and a Timex watch body survived. The remains are up at the holding morgue in Good Sam, so they don't go through the official records until we know what happened."

Willie nudged out his chin, signaling for Hooker to share the rest.

Hooker looked down at his hands—picking at each

other's cuticles. His lips were drawn back tight against his teeth.

The Squirt cleared his throat, and Maddie drew her eyes to the young man. He squirmed on the chair. "There was more."

"More bodies?" She shot Hooker a hard frown.

"No, not bodies—bags." Hooker looked up and looked soft at the Squirt for his support. "There were four dive bags full of stolen loot."

"Money?"

Hooker shook his head and reached in his pocket. He placed the large scarab on the table next to the watch. Slowly, Maddie frowned and picked up the artifact. Her eyebrows rose as she felt the weight of the gold statuette. "This is Egyptian..."

"Stolen from the Rosicrucian Museum in 1953," Hooker finished.

She gave Hooker a schoolmarm look. "Do you know that for a fact?"

"I talked to them a few days ago. At first, they didn't want to admit it, but eventually, we came to an understanding."

She studied the young man's face. Softly she asked, "Which would be...? I mean, after all, it is stolen goods."

Hooker scooted his chair a tiny bit to face her more directly. "Yes, well... there was a problem with complacency. No collusion, just not the due diligence in the job the person was tasked to."

He rolled his upper lip in and bit it in an attempt not to smile. "The long and short of it is, they will be eventually happy to replace a gallery of forged items for their real possessions, as long as there is no publicity or official involvement. They don't know how I came by it all, not about the bodies or anything else. And, I get the feeling they don't want to know."

Maddie's hand came to rest on the table with more of the weight of the circumstance than the gold bug. Her eyes slowly closed. "And Danny was involved..."

Willie put his arm around her shoulders. "It would appear so Mads. It would appear so." He looked across at Hooker. Their lips were mirrors as they drew tight against their teeth. There was nothing easy or warm and fuzzy about the whole mess.

Maddie's index finger rotated the gold bug in a slow circle. "So, Hooker... where do we go from here?"

"I was hoping you could help us with that."

There was a challenge and a mystery to solve. Hooker could see the spark galvanize the more intellectual part of her. She sat up and pushed the gold bug back to Hooker.

Hooker took out a piece of paper. "The car was a 1937 Chevy Master Deluxe. It had a Lincoln straight-eight stuffed in it. The back seat was a bucket chest partitioned off for running what looked like boxes of shine. Probably gallons would be my guess. The depth wasn't right for tall bottles, and the buckets looked like they were split into squares."

He looked over his notes. "We found a plate, and it came back registered to a Giovanni Pappas in Salinas." He glanced up to note her looking at Willie. Returning to his notes, "The county records had a Giovanni Michelangelo

Pappas of Salinas pass away on the ninth of June in 1959. It seems he was survived by his wife and half of the population of the Salinas area." Hooker looked up.

Maddie and Willie both burped a small laugh at the same time. "As long as you were Greek or Italian, you were related to a Pappas. There were Pappas everywhere."

Willie continued the litany. "If you kicked over a rock, or turned over a wash pan, there was a Pappas underneath." He winked.

Maddie lowered her eyelids to half-mast. "Half the girls Danny, Ben, or Randy dated in school were Pappas." She turned to look at Willie.

Willie leaned back with his hands in front of his chest. "Whoa there, Nelly, there were none I knew of in those days," alluding to his being gay, "but there were a few I had wished were..." He smiled a lecherous grin.

She feigned disgust and backhanded his belly. "You are so disgusting some days, William." She turned and smiled with a wink at Hooker the Squirt could also see. Never lovers, but always best friends and soul mates bonded for life.

Maddie reached her hand out. "Do you have an address there?"

Hooker pushed it over. She looked it over and showed it to Willie with a frown. "That was out in the backyard, wasn't it? On the back way toward Hollister?"

Willie pulled on his pursed lips. His fingers rubbed on the stubble he hadn't shaved that morning. Hooker could hear the soft sandpaper sound. "Maybe... there was another road, too, that we used to take it ran straight into the airport..."

Hooker could tell from experience the two were about to start wandering down memory lane, and the next thing mentioned would be this car or that. He glanced at his watch. "We have to go soon and get some paperwork from the Fly before she leaves. She's got two tows to come up from Salinas by the end of the weekend, so we'll get paid to go down and snoop a bit."

"Do you remember any people Danny hung around with when he was in town?"

Maddie blinked a few times. "Umm... no... not offhand. But if you're going down, why don't you stop in and see Ben. If anyone can remember who Danny was hanging out with, he would be the one to remember."

Hooker took back the paper and stood along with the Squirt. They both stretched and yawned with a smile. The Squirt voiced their twin feelings. "Man, I could get used to this kind of day."

Hooker smiled. "Just remember, as soon as they have the hours of practice they need, the massaging stops."

The Squirt pulled a small yellow piece of paper from his pocket and smelled it as he smiled at Hooker. "Or not."

Hooker just rolled his eyes and looked accusingly at his uncle. "He must get that behavior from your side of the family."

They all laughed as Maddie leaned in for a hug from first Hooker and then the Squirt. "It's good to see you up and getting around, John. Which reminds me... "

"I know. I still owe you a paper on the Federal vs. State codes for firearms."

She patted his chest. "Good boy, I expect all five pages typed by Wednesday dinner."

Hooker frowned but didn't ask. He knew Maddie knew the Squirt would be at Dolly's for Wednesday dinner.

CHAPTER FIFTEEN

M AE IDLED ON the shoulder of the narrow two-lane country road. The only indication it was a majorly used back road was the stripe in the middle had been repainted in the last ten years, at least. There were still fades of a thicker, brighter white.

Hooker looked out his open window to the house and barns across the street. The house could have passed for an old Victorian farmhouse somewhere else, but to Hooker, it just screamed fresh as the houses on Stupid Hill. He made a mental bet with himself that there was a master suite taking up almost the entire second floor.

"Is it just me, or do the house and barn look disgustingly new and a little large for a truck farmer?"

Hooker looked over at the kid with a raised eyebrow. "A little hinky even to you, too?"

"Well, it's not like they are pot growers or something. That would be a little bold, even way out here, but the house is at least forty feet by fifty feet across and even has a third floor. So even without a basement, we're talking a farmhouse at well over five thousand square feet. Even if they're Mormons or Catholics—it's one big house."

Hooker looked back at the building in question. "Manny and Stella's house is 4,000 on the main floor and almost that much in the basement. And it was built basically for just the two of them."

"No, it wasn't."

Hooker looked back at the kid with a furrowed brow.

The Squirt shrugged. "It wasn't. I've seen the original plans and talked to Stella about it. Originally, they built your suite for his father and mine for an around the clock nurse. The downstairs was always about storing the tons of canned goods she puts up every year for the relief pantry for cops and such. They always planned on a three-car garage, and what is now Candy's apartment was going to be an office if the pantry ever needed one."

Hooker slowly remembered something along those lines being mentioned over the years. "So now we're building a big barn out in the hill just so all of the pantry stuff can be out there."

The kid shrugged. "It makes sense if you think about it. Every year, Stella and others spend days setting up the tents and stoves and such for canning literally tons of fruits and vegetables as they're harvested or gleaned from the fields. But now there will be a permanent row kitchen along the one side. The only thing not permanent will be the processing tent, and even that could be made as a gazebo. But the seventy-five hundred square feet of warehouse barn is the biggest thing. I don't even want to think about how much food can be stored there and stacked sixteen feet high."

Hooker nodded his thumb back out the window. "But it still wouldn't explain this house or what is built to look like a large horse or cow barn with an oversized hayloft on a truck farm."

The Squirt looked again at the document from the highway patrol. "But this is the address for old Giovanni."

Hooker flicked the door handle and pushed the door with his boot. He nodded his head at the Squirt. "Well, kid, we aren't going to get answers just sitting here."

Hooker left Mae in a low rumble as their four boots hit the ground. As they walked down the middle of the road away from Mae, the area's silence took over. Mae became only a distant white noise as they turned into the long driveway.

Hooker walked slowly with his head down like a tired worker. The Squirt was a mirror image. Both sets of eyes were looking around. Softly, Hooker mumbled, "Notice anything?"

"Like the fact the dirt in these fields hasn't been turned in a few years?"

"That would be it."

As they approached the house, a large man stepped out through the side screen door. He eyed the two and the large tow truck parked on the highway. "What can I do for you, fellas?"

Hooker looked up with a jerk, feigning surprise. "Oh, hey... hi." He pointed his left thumb back over his shoulder. "We towed a truck the other day for the county, and the address it was registered to was here. It was kind of old, but we have to get an owner's sign-off to collect the tow fees from the county." He pulled a slip of paper from his jacket pocket. "Are you Mr. Giovanni Pappas?"

The man couldn't figure out what was off, but he did know he was not the guy they were looking for. He stepped close to the screen door. "Hey, Fred, do you know a Geo-something Papa?"

"Giovanni," Hooker corrected him.

A scrawny guy with a gray complexion opened the door. "Who?"

Hooker studied the new guy, and then dumbly squinted at the name on the paper. "A Giovanni Papa or Pappas," he looked up expectantly.

The man thought for a moment. "You must mean old Gino. He sold the place. Well, his daughter sold the place back in 1959 or 1960."

Hooker swore and pulled his face in a side grimace as he kicked at the dirt and looked at the partially opened door to the barn. He quickly looked down at the paper and then back at the man. "Do you know where I can find his daughter... the one you bought it from?"

A man came down the stairs slowly. "I wasn't here back then. What's this about?"

Hooker wasn't sure he wanted the man too close after what he had seen through the barn door. "Well, the county had us tow an old truck last night. But because the tags had expired, we have to get the owner to sign-off on the tow for a derelict afore the county will pay for it."

The man stopped about six feet from the two. It was

close enough for Hooker. The Squirt was kicking at the dirt and playing at being a step above an inbred drooling basket case. "It weren't no easy tow lass night." Even Hooker wasn't sure if the Squirt had all of his teeth or marbles.

The man rolled his eyes in commiseration at Hooker, who had just dead-panned him. Hooker wasn't going to show much more intelligence.

"I think her name is Corrina or something. Maybe it's Connie. I think she has a beauty salon down at the south end of town. I think her last name is Mannis or something."

Hooker juggled his eyebrows as he shrugged his mouth to one side. "Beauty salon at the south end... How many can there be? Thanks for the help." He turned, and they started walking.

"Hey, what kind of truck is that?"

Hooker looked back with his best deadpan. "It's a tow truck." He blinked a few times as he watched the man decide if Hooker's answer was the most intelligent he was going to get out of the two.

He waved. "Well, you boys have a good day." He turned back to the man still on the porch, and as he climbed the stairs, he smiled at the other and muttered, "Stupid fucking Okies."

As Hooker and the Squirt climbed in the truck, Hooker took one last slow look over the entire spread. No crops had grown there since the house was built. He hit the big yellow brake release and jammed the gears into fourth as he glimpsed the two men still watching from the porch. He purposely ground the gears going into the next three gears.

As Mae picked up speed, and they were a half-mile

down the road, the Squirt closed his eyes and then looked over at Hooker. "Did you see the lights in the barn?"

Hooker nodded. "That small shed on the side where the power lines came in, it was a commercial 440-volt feed. The shed holds a step-down converter. They're using a lot of power to run a whole lot of lights." He looked over at the kid. "I don't think they are growing string beans."

The Squirt gave a low whistle. "Did you notice there were more than a few door panels cut in the end about fifteen feet up on the barn?"

Hooker thought a moment and then nodded. "I wonder if there is a second floor, too."

The Squirt ran his thumb and forefinger along his pursed lips. His eyebrows rose as he weighed the concept of a double-decker pot-growing barn. "The building is probably bigger than a Safeway. That's a lot of dope."

Hooker yawned and smacked his lips. "Let's go see if we can find a beauty salon owned by a Connie Mannus or something. And then we can get some lunch before we go see Uncle Ben." Hooker gave the Squirt a hard look. "You don't ever want to be on the receiving end of Ben's cooking."

"Is that why he's still a bachelor?"

"No. And if we are lucky, he might have had a bath this week."

"Ewwww." The Squirt threw his head out the window for some feigned fresh air. Hooker just laughed, but not hard. He knew the truth about Maddie's absent-minded genius brother.

There were three beauty salons in just as many blocks. The one in the middle was the one they were looking for.

Carla Minton was Gino's step-daughter and sole heir. She had sold the farm in 1959 and never looked back.

The bleached blonde with the scary bee-hive hair-do and a mouth full of gum was just as snappy as her gum. "That farming shit just wasn't my thing." Her gum snapped. "My mama took to that shit like a..." She turned and pointed the scissors in Hooker's direction. "Well, like a pig in shit. She and Gino were two peas in a pod. She loved running the farm, and he loved eating her cooking. He loved making the shine, and mama was an alcoholic." She put her turned-in wrist on her hip as she looked at the stoic woman's hair. "Hell, so am I... but at least I go to meetin' once in a while to keep me on the straight and narrah."

She made the last snip on the woman's hair and patted her on the shoulder, bending close and almost yelling. "Madeline, y'all can go sit under the dryer for twenty minutes. I'll blow you out then."

The small bird lady with a full head of shoulder-length hair got up and tottered past Hooker. As she passed, she leaned in near him. She muttered softly out of the side of her mouth. "Crazy fucking bitch thinks I'm deaf... but she is the best stylist in town."

"Madeline, now you go on now. Leave them young boys alone. They be much too young for you." The blonde pushed the broom around, catching up the small pile of gray hair on the floor. She stopped and leaned against the chair. "Now, which one of you is next?"

The Squirt closed his eyes feigning sleep but knew he would be the sacrificial lamb. The silence stretched then he heard Hooker take his leather jacket off and ease into the seat.

"Just a little off the ears. But not white sidewalls."

She snapped a fresh apron and draped it over him. Pulling the strip of paper around his neck, she settled into the routine of a barber. "So, what did you want to know about old Gino for?"

Hooker went for the upfront approach. "We found his old car."

Snap! The gum had not even exceeded her mouth—she was an inside the mouth popper—a very loud, inside the mouth popper. "Which one? He had a bunch of them. Parked them all over, left the key in them, and just forgot where they were. I don't think he ever paid more than fifty clams for one." *Snap!* "One day, he came out of a store and got into a car. The key was in it, so he knowed it was his. Just drove off home." *Snap!* "The police came and got their patrol car about an hour later. I think it took the police chief that long to stop laughing."

Hooker chuckled as she snipped and snapped. "This was a 1937 Chevy Master Deluxe. The back seat was rigged to run shine." He was hoping this detail would produce some special pay dirt.

SNAP! She laughed and held onto his shoulder with both hands as she crossed her legs to keep from peeing herself. "Honey, they was all rigged for running shine. Even his three John Deere tractors had a stash box."

Hooker groaned. "So you probably wouldn't remember who might have borrowed the car to run some shine up to San Jose." He turned and looked at her.

She took his head in both hands and gently turned it back. The snap of her gum was quiet and contemplative. She snipped silently. "Half the county knew the cars had the keys in them, so they just used them as they needed. But the only people I can think of who would borrow one to run shine up to the cities would be maybe his nephew, Harold... but he blew out of this town a long time ago."

"How long ago?"

She stopped and rested her hands on his shoulder. "Oh, hell... must have been about the time I started getting serious with my husband... so about the end of the war. That's the Korean War."

Hooker waited. "So about 1953?"

She held a mirror in her hand at her hip. "Well, my Sarah Lee was born in August of '54, so... yeah, sometime in the fall of 1953 would be about right. Why?'

"Do you know if he knew a Daniel Robinson?"

She had started to hold a mirror up for Hooker to look at her work. Instead, she sat heavily down in the next chair. The wind was taken from her. "Oh, my... Now there is a name I haven't heard in a long time. Danny Robinson." She sat stewing in many mixed memories rushing back. Hooker watched her face.

"Danny was one hundred and ten percent pure steaming, sweaty, make you go change your panties after third period, kind of hunk. He was a few years ahead of me in school, but I wasn't the only girl in town who would have let him do what he wanted in the back seat of a car." Hooker could tell he had hit some kind of pay dirt. He just had to wait it out. The woman sat in her own dreamland. "He was the captain of the football team and would wear his jacket with the big red 'S' on the side. All of us girls just knew it stood for sex because nobody thought he would stop at just a kiss and some titty rubbing on a Friday night."

She looked up slowly as she struggled her way back. The blush started on her chest and didn't stop as her mind pushed the blood harder and higher. Hooker didn't smile. He wasn't going to taunt. She fanned her hands in front of her face and her exposed chest. "Oh, my."

"So you knew him." Hooker wanted to roll his head in a brainless zombie move, but he knew the behavior was restricted to home. "Do you have any idea who he used to hang out with in the fifties?"

"Sure, that's easy. He hung out with his company in Korea. He was in the reserves—Army, I think. When Korea started up, they all became active and were gone."

Hooker slowly slid the apron off his neck. He ran his hand around his head and looked in the large mirror. He glanced with a small smile at the bird lady humming happily to herself under the dryer. *Damn, the old lady was right—she really is good.*

"What was he doing before Korea?"

"I think he was driving stuff around."

"You mean moonshine?"

The infectious blonde laughed in a husky tinkle. "Well, shine too, but I seem to remember him hauling produce and anything else needed. We didn't have all the Mexicans back then, and a lot of the Okies and Arkies you wouldn't trust to drive your little girl's tricycle. So, a guy like Danny who could drive anything was in demand."

"Was there anyone he drove with or drank with?" Hooker was trying to get a feel for how old Carla actually was at the time. With the bleached blonde hair, it was hard to peg how old she was now.

"There were a couple of boys from the other Pappas families. But I couldn't tell you which. In fact, they might have been one of the Greeks. I just wasn't paying attention to other boys by then. As I said, I was already a unit short of a husband, and none of the field guys were going to get me the house I wanted."

"House?"

"You know... the American dream. White picket fence, a house at the end of the block, car in the garage..."

Hooker nodded. "Speaking of houses... have you seen the house and barn the new people built on your uncle's old place?"

She rolled her eyes and leaned in toward Hooker. "You mean the ones you never see?" She winked slowly. "Some say there are times at night if you stand along the road, and the breeze is just right... you don't need no shine to light up your night."

Hooker rolled his lips in toward his teeth and nodded. "Yeah, that's what we were thinking, too."

"So... Why all the questions about Danny anyway?" She stood and laid the hand mirror on the side counter. Turning, she looked from the Squirt to Hooker. "What's he up to these days anyway?"

Hooker bit down on his lips. The Squirt blinked slowly and said, "He's dead. He died in 1953 as best as we can tell."

Her face drained, and she stumbled to hold onto the one chair. Her breath was one long, "Nooo."

Hooker put his hand on her shoulder and guided her to sit in the chair. "There were four bodies. We're trying to figure out who the others are."

"Oh, my."

"OH, MY?" BEN laughed. "That's all she had to say?"

Hooker was thankful they had caught Ben wet and with only a towel around him. The house was another matter. Hooker told Ben he should get some fresh clothes on and that they'd be waiting out on the side porch where the refrigerator was. The one habit of Ben's Hooker liked was his penchant for root beer. The old Frigidaire had three pull spigots coming out of the door—draft root beer, moonshine, and milk.

Hooker swallowed another large mouthful of root beer. "Pretty much. I think she was pretty shaken."

Ben put his fingers and thumbs to his pursed lips and stroked the top of his nose with the side of his index finger. His eyes were pointed out across the freshly turned fields, but Hooker could tell his sight and mind were twenty years away.

Hooker looked over at the Squirt, who was in his own world as he studied the barn and tilled earth of a true working farm. Small farms like Ben's were the backbone of the entire Salinas area. Generations of families had struggled to carve out a livelihood from the earth. Hooker finally saw what the Squirt was focused on. In one distant corner was a large live oak tree. Underneath, Hooker could see the small white chunks of marble and granite. They were headstones from generations past on the family homestead, marking heritage, as well as a signpost for the next generation.

Hooker leaned toward the Squirt and asked quietly, "The cemetery?"

The Squirt nodded. "It must be strange, and yet comforting to know you are living where generations of your family also stood, lived, worked, had children, and finally died."

Hooker thought about his life in the foster system and how it mirrored the Squirt and his sister Candy. Handfuls of years also meant handfuls of new homes. With them, there were no roots. They didn't even know who their parents had been. Hooker thought about his sister. *I don't even have a real sister. At least the kid has Candy.*

Hooker confided in the kid. "The most recent stone out there is a guy named Jethro, and he was buried in 1912. Died of an acute case of lead poisoning..."

Ben harrumphed and then started laughing. "He got all six lead poisons from the mayor, and then the mayor calmly reloaded and put all six in his wife. After that, he went outside and unloaded six more shots in old Jethro's flivver." Ben waved his hand out toward the cemetery. "If'n you want it, the car is buried right next to old Jethro. I guess, to the family, it just seemed fittin' somehow."

The Squirt thought about the car being buried with the man. And then he remembered this was a family who not only farmed, but also made and ran moonshine, and built very fast cars, raced many, and sold even more. His right cheek pulled back in a smile as his head rolled left to look at Hooker, who was also nodding at the logic of it all. The old flivver and where it ended up, summed up the entire make-up of the family, from Maddie on back.

Hooker got up and pulled himself some more root beer. Turning, he blew the foam head into the yard. "Do you remember who Danny used to hang out with after WWII?"

Ben sipped on his mug and thought. "Probably one of the Pappas kids. They were all younger than he was, but he wasn't much about age differences. There used to be a whorehouse out on the road down to Monterey. The summer before he went into high school, he walked in and looked at all the young fillies. They were all about five or ten years older than him. Then he walked over to the madam. He whispered in her ear, and she was his every Saturday afternoon for a couple of years. Never charged him, neither."

The Squirt leaned forward to look at Ben. "What did he whisper?"

Ben hiccupped a snort. "Told her he was about to turn eighteen and was a virgin. He wanted someone to teach him the ways of women." He looked down the porch and smiled a silly grin at the Squirt. "By the time she figured he was only thirteen, she knew he had balls of brass and cast iron, and it didn't matter anymore... she was in love." He leaned back in the rocker and chuckled at the old times and his brother's shenanigans.

Hooker wondered if Maddie knew the story. "So which

Pappas do you think he might have been close enough to in 1953 to go get in some trouble with?"

Ben was still. His focus was across the field and back in his youth.

Hooker watched. The man could have been a statue. His shirt didn't rise and fall, like other people when they would breathe. Hooker knew this man breathed shallow. It came from tending a wood-burning still for years. Hooker watched the slight flare of the man's nostrils as he thought. This was the same as Manny playing classical music with his large headphones on.

Slowly, the statue turned his head. "Two people... but they won't do you any good."

"Why?"

"They're gone."

"Moved away gone, or dead?"

The older man shrugged and stuck his lower lip out. "Hard to say."

"So who, then?"

"Hank and his little sister... Mary or Terry, or something." He stood up, scratching his butt through his denim. He splashed a little from each of the pulls on the cold box, swished it around in his mug, and threw the liquid mix out into the yard.

Putting the mug back on the shelf turned down, he slowly backed up and leaned his butt against the railing. He washed his hands along the stubble on both sides of his face. Hooker could hear the sandpaper from his chair.

"Hank and he used to haul a lot of everything all over the valley. There was always a demand for someone who had the intelligence to drive four gears, six tons of produce, and get there safely. Hank was another one. Both were good at the racetrack over Hollister way, too." He looked up and smiled. "Not as good as Maddie, but then, not even dad had her kind of heart. We always joked about the reason she could drive so fast was she didn't have any balls to get in the way." He chuckled at times gone by when his kid sister was the fastest woman on four or two wheels.

"The two of them never cared whose car or truck or tractor they were driving. If it had tires and an engine, they had it figured out. Hay, machinery, turnips, or shine, they just didn't care. It was just another chance to drive something and make some money." He looked over his shoulder at the fields and distant road where a red truck was driving by. His voice tapered off, "If it was trouble, it was most likely with Hank."

"So what happened to Hank?"

"Nobody knows." He buzzed his lips against his teeth and then made them into duck lips and blew a raspberry as he still processed his memories. "It was a big mystery around these parts. There were three or four of them... just disappeared one day. Nobody heard anything ever again from none of them."

"What about the sister?"

Ben's eyebrows rose as he looked back at the peeling paint on the clapboards of the house. "Now, there was an interesting one. Quite a looker, kind of like a Jane Russell sort of gal. She wasn't small but just nicely curvy in the right way. You could tell she had spent her time in the fields like most of us.

"She took it hard about her missing brother. After a short while, she quit her job and pulled up stakes. All of us kept waiting to see her in a movie or something. She was good looking. In fact... now as I think on it, I think she and Danny had a thing going before he shipped off to Korea."

"But he never came home."

The man shrugged his face and put out his palms. "That's what we always thought."

The Squirt was processing all of the information. One of the items floated to the top of his bubbling stewpot. He leaned forward. "Did any of the stuff on the missing guys ever make it into the papers?"

Ben fluffed his lower lip. "Sure, the Salinas paper at least. A couple of guys go missing in a small town? That will always sell papers."

Hooker stood and looked out at the afternoon sun. It was lighting the way toward dinner.

As Mae rolled, the Squirt looked over thoughtfully. "We know all of the bodies were male... What if?"

Hooker flipped the toggle and moved the gear shifter into the next level of gears. Mae surged down the highway. It had been a long day, and Hooker was hungry for crab. His lips drew in and played around his teeth. "Okay, let's say she was with them. Why would she survive, and they didn't?"

Hooker knew the Squirt had looked up what a 1937 Chevy Master Deluxe looked like. Hooker had an idea, but he also had looked up the boxy sedan. The car was what today would be called a 'stand-up' kind of car, as in you could almost stand up in it. Its high body profile put a lot of weight at the top, which made it easy to tip over. Hooker knew a lot of the old gangsters would put large engines in them not to necessarily go faster, but to go fast with the extra half-ton of weight welded onto the frames near the ground. Later in the fifties, people like Maddie and Ben learned to lower the tops, and also make the suspension only react so far by welding in anti-sway bars. They also learned about heating the springs to lower the bodies. But the Master Deluxe they had recovered had none of that. It was just a straight-up utility moonshine runner with a fast mill—a gentleman's highway car.

Hooker could sense the Squirt lean back and smile as he relaxed and laid his elbow out of the window. He had tossed the car in his mind and had an answer.

Hooker waited and then couldn't, "Aaannd...?" He looked over at the smug young man.

"She was thrown out in the first set of rolls. The car rolled to the passenger side first, which locked the guys in, but popped the driver door."

"Then why wasn't the fourth guy, the one who was sitting behind her, thrown out also?"

"Because he was busy being the projectile killing the guy in the front seat. He was the large blow that broke Danny's neck."

"Why not the girl?"

"Because she was the only one who had something to hold onto... the steering wheel. That makes her the driver."

Hooker thought about it. No matter how he tossed it in his mind, the kid had gotten there ahead of him. He looked over and smiled at the kid.

As Hooker set the brakes and let Mae rattle down to silence, he petted Box's ear as he looked out at the large sheds of Cannery Row. His eyes drifted closed as he slowly drew in the smells of the ocean, fishing boats, and rotting kelp and other things making the area so special. He kicked open the door. "Crab for dinner, Box."

He didn't have to tell his orange partner twice about food. They all slid out of the truck and locked the doors.

Coming around the front of the giant truck, the two leather-clad men walked, bracing the large orange cat with one eye, one ear, and plenty of scars. The smell of potential drew them to dinner on the wharf with a seat by the sea.

Later, as they sat on the edge of the wharf hanging their legs over the sea lions lounging below, Hooker sucked on his fingers. "Even if she was the driver, how would we find her twenty years later in a place as big as Los Angeles? I sure as hell won't be getting a tow down there to go snooping around."

The Squirt split open his third lobster and drew out the meat. "I've been thinking about that." He dredged a thumb-sized piece through the cup of butter and slurped it in his mouth. His eyes closed as he chewed leisurely, savoring each little burst of flavor. Hooker almost laughed, but he remembered his first time, too.

Hooker looked out at the sunset shooting orange and red rays mixed with the still strong white light limned the small cloud hiding the sun. He slipped Box another finger of crab onto his paper. The cat hadn't stopped purring rough and loud since they set foot on the wharf.

The Squirt unabashedly made rude sounds as he

sucked his fingers clean and leaned back. "I don't think she went that far."

"How far?"

"To Los Angeles—it wasn't her kind of town."

Hooker looked through the shells for any other large pieces of meat, and then laid it all on Box's paper. The furry man could clean the last pieces. Hooker looked up at the Squirt. "Why not? If she's built as Ben said, she could go land a waitress job and get discovered."

"But nobody ever saw her in a movie."

"Okay, so the movies are out. Why is Los Angeles—not her kind of town?"

"Because, for one, it is not a town. It's a city—a very busy, noisy city where she doesn't know anybody." He watched a bird fly by and then land on top of a boat's cabin. He turned toward Hooker. "How many generations do you think are buried out in the old cemetery?"

"The family one? Out at Ben's place? Those aren't his family."

The kid smiled in a lopsided loopy kind of smile. "It doesn't matter. How many generations?"

Hooker looked down the wharf as if there was an answer. He thought about the Californians owning the land in the early 1800s, and Steinbeck's story of the dust bowl fugitives who ended up building the large truck farms scattered across the landscape of the entire Monterey, Salinas, Watsonville, Hollister area, and ran up the 101 to Gilroy and Martinez. He looked back at the kid. "It's a small cemetery, but maybe four or five generations. Why?"

"Which is why she didn't run off to LA. There isn't a family cemetery there."

"But there's one here?"

"It doesn't matter whether there is or not. It's the roots. All of her roots are here. Ben said it showed that she had worked in the fields as a kid. I'm assuming he meant she wasn't scrawny."

"Maddie isn't a beefcake."

"Maddie didn't work in the fields."

Hooker frowned. "How would you know?"

"The way Ben talked about her. She was different, special even. She could outdrive everyone. I'll bet by the time she was old enough to see over the dashboard, she was also the better at turning a wrench, too."

"It still doesn't explain the Pappas girl."

"Sure it does."

"How?"

"Maddie went to college. She was also the fastest woman alive for a while. In theory, she could have raced anywhere. She could have taught or worked in a library anywhere."

"So?"

"She made it as far as San Jose."

"Well, because..."

"Because she married a guy and settled down there? No. Because she followed Willie there? No. Because San Jose made her the best offer? I don't think so."

"Then, why?"

"The cemetery."

"I told you the cemetery isn't theirs."

"Where is the family plot?"

"I think they own some land on Mount Angel."

"Bingo. She is the same kind of person. She's within an hour or so of her roots."

Hooker pinched his fingers to his pursed lips and watched the giant burning ball, silently slip beneath the edge of the world. The last rays of daylight splayed like a giant crown.

The kid was right. Family is a very powerful and compelling thing.

CHAPTER SIXTEEN

THE SQUIRT SQUIRMED as he got back into the truck after they had dropped the tractor. He had been quiet most of the ride back up from Salinas Impound yard. Hooker watched him out of the side of his eye as Hooker checked his mirrors and eased Mae into gear and rolled out of the gated yard. Hooker stopped on the street and went back to close the gate and secure the lock he had the key to. It was only one of seven secure yards Hooker was trusted with a key.

Walking back toward the cab, the image of Box circling his bed at the Romero Hacienda after Stella had washed the cover was exactly how the Squirt was acting. Something wasn't settling with him. Hooker decided to check the tires and give the kid some time. Grabbing the weighted maul, he bounced it along all ten tires as he made the circle of the largest tow truck in the five Bay counties. With a top speed, thanks to the new engine and transmission, of over 150 mph, Mae West was also the fastest tow truck, too. As the motto under her figure painted waving from the engine bonnet said, 'It's what's up front that counts.'

Putting the large hammer back in its hole, Hooker climbed back up into the cab. He put the transmission in gear, hit the air brake release, and eased on down the street as his right hand fell to find empty air where he expected a fuzzy ear. Looking down, as his foot hovered over the brake pedal, he saw the shape of the large orange cat filling the box. The low snore was all he needed in reassurance. Hooker looked up into the face of the Squirt. Both were smiling.

"I think we have a Box with a very happy tummy," Squirt said as he also rubbed his own.

Hooker nodded as he spun the steering wheel through the right and immediate left to get up onto the Almaden Expressway. "Yeah, you weren't too shabby yourself on those bugs and crabs." He smiled. The dinner had cost Hooker almost a third of the tow, but it had been well worth it to introduce the Squirt to eating at the end of the wharf. Watching the sun go down over the Monterey Bay was just the dessert.

Capitol Expressway came up, and Hooker took the cloverleaf and headed east. The Squirt frowned over at his boss. "I thought we were headed home?"

Hooker leaned back tall in the seat as he tried his best imitation of Uncle Willie explaining the facts of life. "Well, John... it's like this. There are some things you should never compromise in your life. Love is one of those. Ice cream is another. And when those two things come together, it's up there with the most sacred of all things."

The kid stuck his hand out into the crisp fall air as he smirked. "It is just the right temperature for some French vanilla."

"Probably just right for even a triple scoop…"

"…in a sugar cone," the Squirt finished. They laughed, and Box just turned over but kept snoring. Hooker knew he would wake up for his dab in the bowl.

Twenty minutes later, as they headed back across the valley on Blossom Hill Road, the Squirt had the bag with the large oversized strawberry and caramel Sunday between his knees. Both windows were open to the night air, and all three tongues were busy with ice cream.

The radio speaker crackled. "Hooker, are you back in the area?"

Hooker passed his cone over to the Squirt and reached behind his head for the microphone. "Yes, I am, Dolly. How can I be of service?"

There was a long pause. "Okay, I'm going to let this one slide because I called you. Please don't talk on the radio around my girls when you are eating ice cream."

Hooker lowered and slowed his speech, knowing all six female ears were now listening to what Dolly referred to as his 'bedroom voice.'

"Gee, Dolly, whatever do you have against my ice cream voice?" He could only imagine the two younger gals squirming in their chairs while trying not to giggle.

"Just get your bodies home. And you need to back Mae into the barn. They need you to play crane or something. Other than that, you aren't even on call. Let the Squirt get some sleep."

"10-4, mama. We're gone."

Not knowing if there was a single car or forty at the bottom of the long driveway running down one side of the Hacienda Romero, Hooker backed down the wide driveway. The width of the driveway and the very large parking lot at the bottom behind Manny and Stella's house was to accommodate Stella's little brainchild that grew into a large monster.

The lower end of the Bay Area is an agricultural mecca. From the few orchards left in the south side of San Jose, down through San Martin and Gilroy and then extending through the golden truck farms of the Hollister, Salinas, Monterey, and Watsonville triangle. The area produced almost a third of California's exportable cash truck farm crops. Stella, years before, asked about gleaning the harvested fields for the left vegetables and fruits. She canned and had ready, food for families of police officers when they were in need. What started as a couple of hundred gallons of canning, with Stella and a few other wives, soon grew into a much larger resource.

When Hooker showed up on the scene, they were already putting up tons of jars. The local growers contributed harvested food that overwhelmed Stella's ad hoc system, so the local cannery in San Jose made the offer to commercially can the bulk with a private label. From trucks delivering on Saturdays and Sundays to the finished cans being loaded into trucks, all of the labor was strictly volunteers. The food now serviced not only any police families, but also fire, city, and county workers as well.

Half-buried in the hillside, they were building a large

barn to hold four times as much food as they were previously able. Facing out over the Almaden Valley and running the full length of the barn was an outdoor kitchen set up for major canning.

As Hooker backed at the acres of the parking lot, there were only eight or ten trucks parked along the side near the house. Hooker saw the large rolling doors were open, so he blew his horn a few sharp blasts and backed to the door.

A large police officer dressed in jeans and a t-shirt stepped out and started waving Hooker in. Finally, with the entire truck inside, the officer held up his hand and clenched his fist for Hooker to stop. Hooker set the brake. He and the Squirt slid out and approached the back.

Hooker smiled and could not resist a tease at the tall, husky Filipino officer's expense. "Geez, James, I don't know what you are doing here. There won't be any food stored here for at least another nine or so months."

The deep voice rumbled through the smile. "Good to see you too, asshole. I see those two-bits they left in you aren't slowing down your mouth any." The three of them had worked the grisliest of the three killings.

The Squirt cleared his throat as he leaned against the back of the tow truck.

James turned. "Oh, and who do we have here? Back from the dead—and looking none the worse for wear." He reached over and shook the kid's hand. "I understand you're starting at the academy soon."

"It looks like it. There is talk that if I can pass my physical after Christmas, they might insert me mid-term in January. Chet, I mean, Captain..."

James interrupted him. "I know Chet." He pointed to the far corner and laughed. "He's the one over there with the plumber's crack and swearing at the copper pipe resisting soldering."

The Squirt smiled and rolled his eyes at the visual. "Well, he's seeing if he can get me some books so I can either catch up or challenge some of the course work."

The officer smiled. "Well, if you can study the same way you worked the burn job, I wouldn't be surprised if you weren't ready in six months. Does that recall thing work with reading books, too?"

"Eidetic memory is sometimes a tricky thing. It works best when there are more senses working than just reading. At the burn site, I could smell the torched metal, the paint, and the burned bodies. There was a very light breeze coming from the southeast. I kept hearing the squawk of the two different radio bands, and I'm especially attuned to Mae West's idle cycle sound." He gave Hooker a hard glare. "Although, with a new engine, her idle is about a hundred RPMs faster, and it's not really smooth like it was before."

James Aligo's laugh was deep and boisterous. He slapped his large hand on Hooker's shoulder. "Willie must be slipping, or you have been hard on the delicate girl."

"Hey, Aligo?"

The three turned to see the county commissioner and former detective partner of Manny's walking toward them.

Hooker smiled. "Hello, Paul. Great to see you doing something productive." They shook hands.

Paul looked around at the large barn. "Who would have ever guessed back when Manny harassed the county about the easement, he would actually be building a barn out here?"

Manny's favorite tool, since his retirement by bullet, was the phone. He heard the county was planning to run an easement through the bottom of his twenty acres. Step by step, person by person, he had worked his way from the lowest to the only person that could stop the easement—his old partner. He had calmly listened to all of the bureaucratic horse shit as he carefully kept track on his yellow pad the name and title of each functionary. The time from start to finish went with a synopsis of the functionary's final offer of what they could or couldn't do. With each call, Manny had asked who the next person up the ladder was that he needed to talk to. He was solicitous and kindly spoken, so help was at hand with the next name and phone number or a transfer.

Brick by brick, he would build his case. He never jumped the chain of command. He never pulled any kind of rank by going directly to his old friend. It wasn't so much about the results, as it was about playing the game. He fought and won each step of the battle.

Finally, he had reached Paul. They had exchanged pleasantries, and then Manny told Paul, nicely, to move the easement because he was going to build a barn where the easement would be, thus diminishing his enjoyment of his private property. When Paul started telling Manny it was out of his hands, Manny turned the phone's handset around and pounded it on a rattling board he had brought into the house specifically for the noise.

When he put the phone back to his ear, his old partner

was now remembering Manny's strong-arm tactics of getting things done. Manny softly sighed and then told Paul he wasn't listening. He then proceeded to read from the four pages of specific names, times, and outcome of each conversation of the day. His tone was soft and metered. In the end, he told Paul his next phone calls would be to his sister-in-law, Dolly at Night Dispatch, and then his lawyer, the most feared shark in the South Bay Area.

He quietly hung up, looked at the clock, and went to make himself a sandwich.

The phone rang twenty minutes later. Paul contritely informed Manny the easement was moved down to the bottom of the hill onto the county property, and Manny had the green light to build whatever kind of barn and corrals he wanted.

The two longtime friends had been laughing about it ever since. Business was business, and friendship was never compromised by it.

"What did you want Mae for, Paul?"

Paul turned and guided them over to some long steel I-beams. "We have this gantry system Willie found up at Alameda air station. Evidently, it was made for moving bombs around during the war, but was never installed." He pointed high on the walls. "We've installed the studs on the walls, but we need to lift the beams into place. We looked at a larger forklift, but they only go up fourteen feet. The spuds are at twenty."

Hooker eyed the steel. "How much does the largest one weigh?"

Paul pointed at the longest beam. "The main is about a buck eighty."

One thousand eight hundred pounds, Hooker thought about the dynamics of the extended boom. "I can get it close, but we'll have to tip one end in and secure it somehow, then continue the lift on a carry trammel." Looking to the ridge beam, Hooker saw a large block and tackle hanging. "What is the block hanging up there for?"

Paul laughed. "Looks. The ridge beam is only stressed for a two-foot snow load so the block wouldn't be good for anything more than maybe five hundred pounds."

Hooker looked about. "We could point tie over on that high beam and then run to the beam and on up to the block. It would be enough for the trammel lift so I can adjust my lift point on the beam."

The Squirt unscrewed his face and opened his eyes. "The load on the tie off on the wall as well as the dead load on the block will be about four-hundred twenty-eight pounds, give or take about twenty." He looked up at Paul and smiled.

Paul looked at him with an open mouth then closed it. "Oh, you are going to be hell on the instructors at the academy."

Hooker smirked. The kid had come a long way since Hooker first met him after sticking a fork through his hand as he tried to steal a dollar off the diner's counter.

The kid turned, still smiling. "I'll get the trammel chains."

About an hour later, Candy walked up behind Hooker and put her arms around his middle as she kissed the back of his neck. "Stella said the chili is hot, and the rolls are about five minutes away from coming out of the oven. All the bathrooms are working down here, so everyone needs to wash up and come topside."

Hooker released the levers on the side of Mae and turned into his girlfriend's hug. "Hello, good looking."

Candy blushed from the top of her nurse's uniform to her hair. "You're just saying that because of the sexy uniform."

"I've always liked you in or out of uniform." Hooker turned to address the rest of the men. His whistle was sharp and reverberated in the empty space. "Chili is in five minutes in the big house, and if you need to call your wife to be able to stay—well, just whimper that Stella insisted. Wash up. There are five bathrooms and four hoses between here and the table."

Candy playfully slapped his chest as he spun her around toward the door. "Oh, you are sure the mean one. There isn't a henpecked man in this lot."

Hooker looked back at all the men as he climbed up into Mae and shut her down. Dropping to the floor, he grabbed Candy by the waist, and they continued out the large door. "There isn't a single married man here either."

She looked back and frowned. Hooker laughed. "Yeah, you can share it around with your classmates on Monday."

She looked at him, and then an evil smile crept across her face.

Hooker looked at the stars and the crisp November night. He felt the warm body that was in perfect step with him. Life was looking good. "I hope you're free for lunch tomorrow."

"Why? I need to study, but lunch sounds good."

"Good. I know a little place I want to take you to right after I spend a little time in a certain library."

"Maddie?"

"No, her hometown."

"Where is that?"

"Salinas. It's down near Monterey and lunch."

The Squirt had been following close behind. He slid up alongside them as he wiggled his eyebrows up and down. "Do I get to come, too?"

Hooker looked over. "Nope, you are taking The Granny Car over for Willie to pamper while you are spending some time with Maddie. Chet said he dropped off a stack of books for you."

"Beans."

Candy reached over and ruffled her brother's hair and smiled. She was starting to like the effect Hooker was having on him. She could have done without Hooker stabbing his hand with a fork, but if that's what it took, so be it.

Hooker steered them up the driveway instead of using the secret stairs and door in the pantry. He always liked walking in through the giant hand-hewn gates letting into the entry patio with the Mexican tiled fountain. The gentle sound of the water calmed him, and it always reinforced in him that he was home, *even if his other home was five miles away at Uncle Willie's place.*

CHAPTER SEVENTEEN

THE QUIET OF the small library harmonized with the two scan readers. The past newspaper had all been photographed and turned into leaves of microfiche. Hooker and Candy had the year, but not the right time, so one started with December and the other with November, and they leapfrogged their way back through the year.

"I think this is it." Candy leaned over to nudge Hooker. She noticed he was looking at the cars for sale section. "I don't think you can still get... what is a Hupmobile?"

Hooker laughed. "What did you find?" He smiled at the freckles scrunched as she looked at the ad.

She leaned back and gave him a one-eyed look. "I'm looking for three missing guys, and you're shopping for cars that don't even exist anymore."

"You knew what you were getting into."

"Right," she ran her fingers up into his hair. "Just don't

start wearing long dresses. They don't look good with the leather jacket."

Hooker chuckled. "Noted."

He read the article she had found. "Okay, so missing since late September." Leaning back, Hooker ran the information through his head. "The war ended at the end of July... so where was Danny for those two months?"

"Do they just one day say 'it's all over. Everybody, go home,' or does it take time to unwind a war?" She raised an eyebrow. "My guess is he was somehow involved in the wind-down."

Hooker looked for the September microfiche folder. He found the last week and slid it into the viewer. He scanned through the front pages. Candy leaned on his shoulder, watching. "Do you think it would have made the headlines? This is all about the war unwinding."

"I would think it would make at least the front..." His finger poked at the glass.

They read an article about three men who went hunting and were presumed dead. Hooker pulled up his notepad and started writing the names Hank Pappas, age 29, Zebulon Nickapopalus age 29, and Paul Giodarno age 32. The rest of the story about going deer hunting in the lower ranges near Big Sur Hooker new to be nothing more than conjecture or pure fabrication.

Candy murmured with her jaw still on his shoulder. "What do you think?"

"I think we found our guys... but who was the driver who dragged them into the cave?"

Candy stuck her finger out and touched the screen

where it read 'Theresa Pappas, sister of Hank Pappas, told authorities they had gone hunting but planned to be back to work the next Monday.'

Hooker nodded. "Bingo—the only person who knew where they really went."

"So we need to track her down."

Hooker looked at his watch. "No, it's time for lunch." He smiled at her and kissed her nose.

"So where is this mysterious lunch?"

Hooker stood and rearranged the microfiche folder and leaves. He stood and smiled. He liked the way she had brought her hair down in a loose fluffy ponytail. It softened her features. "For where, you would have to ask Box because I'm not talkin'."

They rode with her nose against the door's window. "I never knew there was so much farming around here." She turned back and looked at Hooker as Box jumped up onto the sun-drenched dashboard and stretched out. "Box certainly knows all the right places."

"If it were your brother sitting there, he would have been in the Squirt's lap the whole trip. The kid is a real sucker for Box. First Box backs him into a corner, and then they are fast friends. I just don't get it."

"Do you think he will ever warm up to me?"

"Your brother? Nah." Hooker laughed.

Candy looked around the spacious cab. "So you run the heater on high, but you don't roll the window up, and you stick your elbow out... why?"

Hooker looked over as he downshifted. "Are you comfortable?"

"I'm not complaining..."

"Well, there you go. You don't like the window open, but then, you don't have a leather jacket either. So you rolled your window up, and now you are comfortable. My legs are warm, my body is warm, and I have some wind on my face. I'm comfortable. And the Squirt runs the same way. But then, he's also weird... did you know he likes ice cream in the middle of winter?"

She laughed. "French vanilla, three scoops..."

"...in a sugar cone," they finished together.

"He told me about the ice cream. I think it was when he decided he really liked you—fork or no fork."

Hooker groaned. "Will you people ever give it a rest?"

He downshifted three gears and nosed the giant truck into a parking lot between two refrigerated trailers with large crabs painted on their sides. "Welcome to Cannery Row."

"As in John Steinbeck?"

Hooker slid out the door. Opening his arms to help her down as she slid right into him, he laughed. "One and the same."

Box led them down the wharf to the large kettle where the man was boiling the crabs or lobster you chose. His kink-tipped tail was flying like a battle banner the whole way.

Candy hung on Hooker's arm, taking in the sights and smells. "He really does know where he's going. He has walked right past three other..."

"Fishmongers."

"Fishmongers and set a beeline for this one."

Hooker stopped them thirty feet from the man and his kettle. "Watch."

Box approached the Asian man, who, upon seeing the large distinct cat, stopped his usual work and chose a part of a fish. Quickly slicing off a few choice bits of meat, he placed them on a small boat he folded a sheet of newspaper into. He stepped out toward Box and placed the small boat with both hands a foot in front of the cat. Box didn't move, just watched.

The man took a small step back, and then two more. Pressing his palms together, he raised them to his lips. With a fluid movement, Box sat back on his haunches and sat up. His left paw rested on his tummy, and he raised his right as if to wash the top of his head. His paw pads were facing the man, who now bowed deeply in mutual respect. The cat returned the respect and quickly devoured the offering of friendship.

The man watched with a sincere smile and then looked up to find Hooker. The smile grew into a brilliant row of white teeth. "Hooker-san, you grace this old man with your warrior guardian." His vision turned to Candy. He clapped his hands together and bowed. "And this beautiful lady, I can only take as the Squirt's sister. Hooker-san, you are most favored."

"Candy, this is Fuji-san. He is the only person who can feed the mange monster raw fish. Fuji-san, this is Candy, my girl."

The man took her hand delicately with a small shake. "I am honored to meet you. You are as lovely as my lotus blossom wife was."

"Did she die?" The words slipped out before she could stop them.

The solemn man rose back and laughed. "Oh, heavens no. She is now fat like a pig. And that gives me just more to love."

Candy was shocked and then laughed as she turned on Hooker. "Do you nuzzle her neck as well?"

Hooker grabbed his face as he shook his head in mock shame. Fuji laughed even harder.

"Of course he has—Hooker-san is Hooker-san. Makes her laugh and giggle like a little school girl." He waved his palm up and down at her body. "So how did a slender woman like you get his attention, much less his arm?" He leaned in with a mock confidential stage whisper. "The only woman he ever brings is his uncle and the nice Maddie-san. I don't think Hooker is interested in her." He leaned back with the smile of a naughty boy.

Candy leaned into Hooker. "So everyone else has been here but me?"

"Manny and Stella won't travel anymore. But we will be taking some crabs back for them." He smiled. "But right now, you need to pick out your dinner."

She looked in horror at the large glass tanks. Hooker hugged her. "It's okay. Fuji-san, how about four crabs and three bugs."

Candy stiffened in his hug. "What are bugs?"

Fuji held up two large lobsters, smiled, and tossed them into the boiling water. He fished one more and a couple of crabs. Reaching back in among the crabs, he nodded toward the end of the wharf. "You go sit now. Fuji brings when ready. You get your own root beer."

Hooker waved and turned Candy around, and they strolled to the end of the wharf with only a stop for two large root beers.

An hour later, Box lay curled up next to the devastated shells, snoring gently as Hooker and Candy watched the fishing boats returning across the bay. Candy wiggled over closer and rested her hand on Hooker's thigh as she leaned into his shoulder. "It's so peaceful."

Hooker looked across the bay to the north. "When things are not so calm at home, this is the place I think of— to quiet the noise."

She changed positions so she could lay with her head on his lap. "That's why you work nights—for the quiet."

Hooker smiled softly and stroked her shoulder. He knew he didn't have to answer. He could tell she had figured it out about him years ago. It was the same reason she had worked the night shift at the diner.

Just about the time Hooker thought she had gone to sleep, Candy asked, "Where do you think she is—the sister?"

"I think the Squirt has the right thought on it. She's somewhere close. Maybe as far as San Francisco, but probably closer."

"How do we find her?"

"We ask around."

"Hmm." She nodded her head in the way you adjust your pillow. Hooker knew she was going to take a nap.

"If you're going to take a nap, let's go back to the truck so I can join you in the sleeper."

She sat up with sleepy eyes, but with a smile.

The radio crackled, and then Karen's voice came through the speaker. "Hooker, Salinas Impound wants to know if you are snagging the trailer this afternoon."

The radio jarred the two awake, and Hooker reached around the small wall to grab the mic. "Just finished up in Monterey and will be there in about an hour."

"10-4. Have you been eating ice cream? You have the voice going on."

Hooker smirked. Dolly would have his hide, but he knew Karen would never talk. "No, darlin'... This is the real deal."

There was dead silence, as he knew the two daytime dispatchers would be first shocked, and then would turn into two large masses of jiggling giggles. He rehung the mic and swung his legs over the edge of the bed. He looked back as Candy rolled overtaking the rest of the blanket to herself. He reached over and tucked it up around her shoulders.

Slipping into his boots, he moved to the driver's seat and fired Mae West back into life. Slipping her into gear, he eased her out into the large lot and then nosed her out onto the street. As he cleared the main area of Monterey, he pushed the eight-track tape into the slot and turned the volume up for comfortable listening. The boys of Texas were just starting into some clear blue water.

CHAPTER EIGHTEEN

W EDNESDAY NIGHT DINNER was a most unusual affair. For anyone who had ever attended Dolly's usual affairs—this one didn't make sense.

Historically, the table was a mix of males drawn from law enforcement, tow truck drivers, and political figures ranging from city officials to the occasional member of Congress. Dolly's reach was far and wide, and it was all focused on what was good for the running of the sprawling city of San Jose and the areas around, better known as the South Bay Area.

Hooker had become a weekly fixture at the head of the table. Nothing had ever been verbalized or acknowledged, but it was obvious to all Hooker was Dolly's anointed one. Dolly played close to the vest, but it was also a known fact the large lollypop microphone sitting behind her desk was a direct line to no other truck than the eleven tons of Mae West and Hooker's left ear.

The largest standout of the unusual was Willie and Maddie. Neither had much of an interest in the running of the city—other than Maddie being a librarian at one of the county libraries. Willie, retired from the Navy for over ten years, was well past any interest in any kind of politics.

Two of the three highway patrolmen were good friends of Hooker. They were the first clue to Hooker that there would be a meeting after dinner. The 'on medical leave' CHP captain sat in the middle of the table. The other, Micha, was one seat down from Hooker. On any other dinner night, either one would blend in with the mix. To have them both there, along with Willie and Maddie, was the clincher in Hooker's mind. *There had been discoveries made, and movement was in the works.*

The third officer, Steven Huggs—was the almost newbie to the table.

Hooker looked to the Squirt at the other end of the long table, seating five down each side. Hooker could tell he was trying to add up the fact of the four—especially Maddie.

Dolly had been stirring things up a bit by having, first, Micha's wife attend, and then had Candy stand in for Hooker the last time he was in the hospital. But Maddie had them both stumped.

The Squirt looked down the table at Hooker, who just shrugged. As usual, all would be revealed when Dolly decided. With these four, it would be the after-dinner meeting.

Long ago, Hooker had learned from watching Dolly that his job at the table was to listen to the conversations, not necessarily participate. He had watched how she hovered with the coffee carafe or the water pitcher. It appeared she was constantly moving, but it was where or how she was moving that had finally caught Hooker's attention. She could be attentive to a select couple or few if the conversation was of interest and to her advantage to listen in on. Even at almost a quarter-ton of mass, she had the ability to become almost invisible as she moved about the table.

Some nights were functions of small talk where she only learned more about certain men, and other nights were a rich harvest of things outside the gray concrete walls important to her Machiavellian ministrations of the city and county.

Tonight, Hooker could tell by Dolly's smooth flow about the table—it was a night of small talk and fluff. There was talk of the upcoming Thanksgiving slug-fest that started the season of blood on the streets.

Most 'civilians' would talk about the holidays and think of parties and gatherings. Law enforcement and tow truck drivers saw things from the perspective of what happens after the parties and gatherings. The only times of the year rivaling the holiday season were the Fourth of July and the two weekends of Labor Day and Memorial Day.

The little stuff like jump-starting batteries and fixing flat tires were the little things keeping Hooker and the Squirt busy while they waited for a crash involving a big rig truck. There were only a few tow companies in the South Bay who handled big trucks. The stretch of the 101, from the south end of San Jose to Gilroy, known as Blood Ally, was Hooker's domain.

One of the drivers from the north end turned to Hooker. "I understand your buddy officer Aligo just opted to transfer back to King and Story?"

Hooker frowned as he mopped up the last of the spaghetti sauce with the end of the sourdough roll. "Why would James do that? He already has lead fragments floating around in him from the Gun and Knife club."

"The way I hear it, he took it because they were looking to put a K-9 unit in there. So not only does he bump up into K-9s, but he also becomes a sergeant. I think he also speaks the languages, too."

Hooker rolled his head. "He's Filipino, but yeah, I know he speaks Spanish and Tagalog, so Vietnamese wouldn't surprise me." He stuffed the last tiny piece of food in his mouth as he pointed his finger in the air. "I think he was out there for a few years before. Every time he was shot or stabbed, they would ask him where he wanted to transfer to, and he'd tell them he had work left to do. I guess maybe he thinks he has some more work to do out there." Hooker chuckled. "Or it's just too dang boring in the south end. He's like me, a nightcrawler."

Hooker looked out the door into the dark room where Dina and Patty were sitting in their pools of light over the switchboard of snakes in holes. Dina could sense Hooker's look. It was time. Without even looking, she nodded.

A few minutes later, there was a sharp whistle from Dina, and all conversations around the table stopped. It was so sudden, Willie and Maddie were left blinking and wondering what happened. Everyone else knew at the whistle, words were cut-off, half-spoken conversations were finished, and the evening was done.

"Mike, you have a T-wonderful holding at westbound Story at the bottom of the ramp.

"Pete, your backup just went 10-7 for dinner, and the auto club is holding a T-3 for you on North Stevens Creek.

"Lupe, Jose is wondering if you died and went to heaven. There are ten pounds of sausage from Chairamonte's in the fridge unless Dolly has dropped it in your lap." Dolly picked up his plate and substituted the box of meat.

"Don, you are on duty in three more hours. Go get some sleep—and leave your home radio off."

"Steven, there is a fender bender southbound 101 at Kooser. Chip, dispatch asked if you could go take it. Probably a no report, but they want an officer to show up.

"Ace, there is a commercial waiting at the Fly's. Pack your bag. It's going to Bakersfield."

Dolly held her hand on Chet's shoulders. She nodded to Willie, Maddie, and Micha to stay seated. As the drivers and CHP officer filed out, they all got a Dolly hug, and Hooker shook their hands at the front door after he had checked the closed-circuit TV to make sure it was safe. As the more seasoned men walked up to the large steel door, they kissed their two left fingers and touched them to the badge they knew was welded just over the doorknob—badge number 701.

In the ensuing silence of the aftermath and as Dolly rinsed and placed the dishes in the dishwasher, Willie looked over at Hooker. "Well, so this is what lodge meetings look like." He smiled as he knew there was more to the dinner than met the casual eye.

Hooker looked at Dolly, who seemed to be busy and not paying attention to the table. He knew different, as she stopped for a second and then nodded as she resumed her work. Hooker had the go-ahead to reveal the inner workings. Family was family.

"Steven was here about... what? A year ago or two?"

The head and shoulders of the large woman never broke stride. "Seventeen months ago."

Hooker nodded and continued. "It was his first time at the table. Right now, he is up for promotion to sergeant. He's on the list but had never met Chet. He's a good officer, but Chet needed a closer look at the man. Roping Micha into the deal was an extra bonus as they will be sergeants together. The difference will be Micha will now be a senior sergeant." He winked at Chet, who had just had the wind knocked out of his sails.

Hooker looked over at his longtime friend, Micha. "Sorry to step out in front of you in breaking the news, but Bobby Sue looked a little tight in the pants the last time I saw her. Knowing the extra bump in pay is coming will make it easier on the little bump under her shirt." He looked at the wide-eyed officer.

Micha's gaping mouth shut, then he opened it as he leaned forward. "Man, nothing gets past you, does it? We weren't going to tell anyone until she was really showing."

Dolly turned as she dried her hands. "Oh, she's showing, Micha... that is if you're Hooker. He told me last week her scrubs were getting tighter top and bottom, but she wasn't getting a fat neck for him to nuzzle. You don't need a second opinion, not with Hooker and fat necks."

Hooker smirked and hid his face in his coffee.

Chet chuckled. "Anything else on the docket? I mean, all of my secrets are on the table now that you filled Micha in on his new promotion..."

Hooker smiled. "Other than we think Mike is carrying a diamond ring around in his pocket? Or, that Lupe is about to buy in as a full partnership with Jose? No... But I do think Pete might be about ready to get out of towing. He has been tired, and getting him to work evenings on Tuesdays and Thursdays, has been like pulling teeth for the last two years. I don't know what he's been taking, but I'm pretty sure he has been at night school. As for Ace... Ace is just always a good man to fill out the group."

Maddie looked at Dolly, who was now standing behind the Squirt pouring coffee. "And you do this every week...?" Dolly smiled and kept pouring as if to say, *welcome to my world.*

Micha leaned back. "So now that my world is blown apart, what are we four doing here?"

Hooker took the lead. "You four or more specifically, the six of us were the main event." He looked to Chet. "Chet, care to lead off with what you found?"

Chet pulled a piece of paper from his pocket and unfolded it. "Theresa Johanna Pappas moved to Saratoga, where she got a job as a cocktail waitress at first Bill's and then moved up in the world out at the Cats. Her last known address was on Trent in some apartments, which are no longer there. We have her showing eleven weeks of income at the country club and then nothing. It was as if she dropped off the face of the earth.

"Interestingly, a new gal started the next week at the country club and at the Cats with a Social Security number going nowhere. Her name was Danielle Patterson. And the address they both had was to a P. O. Box in Las Gatos. I couldn't find any bank accounts, but then over the years, banks have come and gone."

Maddie mused, "So there is no way to know if this Danielle Patterson is really Teresa Pappas or not?"

"Correct."

Micha looked up. "Unless... she got married under either name."

Willie asked, "County records?"

Micha smiled. "To start, or state—even the state would have a record."

Ever the librarian, Maddie qualified the statement. "As long as they got married in this state. But what if they ran off to Reno to get married?"

The Squirt sat up and beamed. "As I was working on one of the papers last month, I happened across another interesting note. Even if you get married in a foreign country, they will also file a conformed copy of your marriage in the state and county you reside in. So as long as she was still living here, this is where the document would be filed."

Hooker frowned. "What if she lived here and her new husband lived in, say, Contra Costa?"

"Same applies. A conformed copy would be filed in each county and another with the state of California. Otherwise, divorces would be a nightmare."

Micha muttered into his coffee. "They already are. Just ask half of any police force."

Chet nodded sadly along with him. It was a known occupational hazard of being a cop—especially the CHP. The irony of the 'nicknames 'Chips' or 'Chippy' and their connotations for 'chipping' or having sex on the side—was not lost on the rank and file.

Hooker allowed a brief time of reverence then looked at Maddie. "So we now know who and where to look. Could you do that, or should we turn the Squirt loose on bird-dogging her to the ground?"

Maddie looked at the kid. "Run her to the ground, and you're off the hook for research reports until after Thanksgiving. Bring us a valid new address, and I'll let you run naked until next year."

Hooker laughed. "Hell, I want in on that deal." Knowing what was coming next—he fished a quarter out of his pocket and slid it down the table to Willie for the swearing jar. The man just nodded and stuck it in his shirt pocket.

CHAPTER NINETEEN

THE DRIZZLE WAS light as Hooker began dropping the chains and hooks off the Peterbilt that had seen a better day on Monday. Tuesday, it had a problem braking, and the northbound 2:45 Freight Express had sheared off about two feet of the truck's front end. A few more inches and the train would have hit the engine and completely messed up the driver's day. As it was, the guy had gotten a ride to the hospital, but only for a few nicks and cuts and a large headache.

"Hey, Hooker?"

Hooker stood up to watch the small Japanese woman bounce from island to island to miss the puddles. Hooker had once seen a television show about football players training. He snickered to think the woman everyone called 'Fly' would have done pretty well at the tire thing. She made one last hop and was on the large island with Hooker.

"What the hell you doing out in this yuck, Fly? Even Box is smart enough to stay in the cab."

"Dolly said you might be interested in a flip I have up north?" A flip is where there is a tow going out and one coming back from the same area.

Hooker hefted the loose chain into the working bed of Mae. "I'm always interested in a good flip. North, south, east, or west—as long as it isn't too far west."

"I've got a Kenworth salvage who wants to go up to Mendocino and a thirty-two-foot bus coming back down from Sebastopol for Hawkins. I think he's going to turn it into an RV or some nonsense. The bus is in a yard so you can pick it up anytime, but the Kenny wants to be there Wednesday because they are taking the four days for Thanksgiving."

Hooker pulled up the last of the chains and puddled it in the chain locker on his deck. Closing the lid, he turned. "So I can have Thanksgiving up in Marin?"

The woman smiled. "Take your girl. Show her you work for a living. Show her some pretty country and do what you want. What do I care? I'm taking six days and going over to Modesto and play with my granddaughter."

"Where is the Kenny now?"

She waved her hand out toward the south lot. "It's the blue one with the king sleeper. I'll leave the keys and paper-work in your cubby hole. You have all the keys, so take it up when you want."

"I'll talk to Candy. I think the school is closed for the whole week, so we might head up on Monday. I'll let you know so it's cleared."

The Fly was already hopping back across the yard. "It's all cleared, take it when you want."

Hooker smiled as he thought about going up to Marin. Hidden in the hills of Marin County was a place called the Apple Farm. It was owned by Stella's best friend for life—Claire and her husband, Norman. Their house guest was Hooker's sister. Norman Osofsky was a retired psychiatrist, who had specialized in psychotherapy for kidnap victims and other prisoner survivors.

Hooker's sister was also a Claire, but at sixteen, she had become a runaway with a thirteen-year-old Hooker. When they had gotten to San Jose, Hooker had been found by redemption in the form of a man who became Uncle Willie. His sister found her home first on the streets and then within a tribe of beings best described as denizens of the night. To save her life, Hooker, and others had staged her death. After some time in a hospital bed, she was released into the care of the Osofskys.

The mind is a fragile organ. Nobody knows how resilient Hooker's sister is, but if need be, she has a permanent home available to her at the Apple Farm—a home as caring and open as the two homes Hooker split his time between. The brief visit with Candy a couple of months before had been a delicate bonding between the two women, and Hooker looked forward to them having some more time together.

Hooker climbed up into the cab of Mae West only to be staring at the single eye of a very large cat standing on the expansive dashboard. Hooker just laughed. "Okay, okay, I'll take you over to the lawn at the school."

The gigantic engine revved as Hooker slipped in the gears, released the brakes, and nosed the truck out of the muddy yard. Rolling down the back streets into the Willow Glen side of the Almaden Expressway, Hooker ran his hand over Box, still standing guard and a reminder to Hooker he needed some lawn.

Hooker never subjugated the standing of the cat or his preferences. Hooker liked French vanilla triple-scoop ice cream in a sugar cone, Box wanted lawn. Don't try to make Hooker eat Rocky Road or pistachio, and Box won't go near mud. It's not the wet because he loves to be in the really hard rain and roll in sprinklers on the grass—it was the dirt or, more specifically, the cliché clay mud sticking to his fur and especially gets up between his toes.

Hooker opened the door, and the orange streak flew through the opening. Hooker pulled the air brake knob and rolled out of the cab. Pulling the lead hammer from its hole, he started banging it on the tires to check for a flat or slow leak. By the sound alone, he could tell if a tire was just a few pounds low. The routine was several times a day. It was also a time for Hooker to think.

He was mulling over things Ben had talked about, and what the Squirt had said about family. Hooker only had Claire or the Mouse, as she had become known as, for the last ten years. They had been fostered kids together in a broken system who ended up selling them from abuser to abuser or pedophile. When they had finally run away, they ended up back together and ran as the only family they knew. When Hooker had been taken in by Willie, Claire had made it known to Hooker she knew where he was, and she was close by. Over the years, they stayed in touch through the underground telegraph of the homeless, the street urchins, and the denizens of the night. There was always some sort of connection.

Now she was only a hundred miles away or at the end of a phone call. She wouldn't talk on the phone, but Hooker could talk through Claire and Norman so there was contact —but she never seemed so distant.

Hooker glanced at his watch and noted the time. Turning, he called for Box. "Come on, Box, let's go pick up your boyfriend." Hooker still wasn't sure how he felt about the usually picky cat taking to the Squirt by the second day. They even put up with each other enough to sleep together, something Hooker would not do, as the cat had a habit of pushing Hooker out of bed or at least taking the pillow and three-quarters of the bed. Hooker had taken to closing his door, but the Squirt and Box seemed to find an agreement about sharing a bed, a couch, or even the sleeper in the truck.

Willie's boyfriend, Hank, had a feeling Box understood the Squirt needed a friend who was physically there for him. The cat filled the need. After all, the Squirt had initially started into the family when Hooker stabbed his fork through the Squirt's left hand, and then a week later, the two of them got shot full of dimes by a crazed killer with a shotgun—after that, sleeping with a cat didn't seem so weird.

Hooker closed the door behind the bounding feline. Box stepped up onto the passenger seat and shook like a dog. Hooker laughed as he was certain the Squirt wouldn't check the seat before he sat on the wet. "What? I don't let you beat up any dogs for a few months, and so you're going to start pulling pranks on poor Squirt?"

The cat looked at Hooker with a slow blink of his one eye. It was as close to the zombie head roll Hooker would ever get from the cat.

The large truck nosed out of the school parking lot and headed for the county hall of records.

"SURE. WHEN DO WE LEAVE?" Candy sat on Hooker's lap.

Hooker stared at Manny, who raised his hands up with palms out. "Don't look at me. You kids are over twenty-one and on your own. You both have keys and your own diaper drawers. I'm just a fly on the wall."

The three younger people at the table all laughed. Stella rose to hide her smile. She had never felt so full. A few months before, she felt blessed to have part of Hooker for a son. Now she had a daughter and parts of two boys.

She stacked the plates on the counter. Turning, she leaned against the sink. "How much would you lose if you took off the week?

"A few hundred, but being Thanksgiving week—maybe more."

"How much for the flip?"

"Six hundred and forty, but because it's not through Don, I get it all, less expenses. Fuel will be about two hundred, and about two hundred should go into the tire fund, so it's about a wash."

Manny joined in. "Have you talked to Don?"

Hooker looked back at Manny. "Checked in this afternoon. He's got a new guy he wants to run hard for a week and see if he can really do backup for me, so this week would be a good trial."

Manny rolled forward on his elbows and lifted his butt off the seat pad of his wheelchair. It wasn't about cooling his ass, as much as a physical manifestation of the ex-detective shifting mental gears. He dropped back down and leaned back. "What did Dolly think?"

"She'll miss me on Wednesday night for dinner, but she had decided to have the girls bring their husbands and Karen's kids for a full Thanksgiving dinner. She was going to invite Willie, Hank, and Maddie too, but I reminded her they would be here the next night along with the Sweets and a bunch of others. But as for towing, she was fine. Jose has a new Trail-All so he could flat-bed any large tractors—he just can't do any recovery so the chips would have to call down Tri-Counties for anything big."

Candy nuzzled into Hooker's neck. "So we can go for the whole week?"

"Do you have any homework?"

She slumped. "Spoiled sport. Of course, I do, and I'll take it."

Hooker looked around at the Squirt. "Speaking of homework..."

The kid sat up. "I have a few possibilities which are looking good." His eyes rolled up in his head for a moment. Hooker knew he was looking at the image of whatever he was recalling. The kid's photographic memory was a blessing as well as a curse.

The Squirt's voice took on the slight difference Hooker was coming to recognize as his robot reading the images in his brain voice. "There is a William B. Gaddis of Santa Clara who married a Daniela Quimms of San Jose, and they are now living in Fremont. There is a Feldman Yurin Slovinotskia who married a Danita Esperanza, and they still live in Los Gatos. Monty P. Helmand married Donna Schmitz, and they are in Willow Glen Cemetery—a car crash. And then there is a guy who married a woman named Dani, spelled Dani. I'm trying to track down more recent information."

Hooker laughed. "You are so full of bull pucky, Squirt."

"Why?" The kid looked hurt.

"Who names their kid Yurin?" Separated out, all five got the joke and laughed.

CHAPTER TWENTY

T HE SQUIRT SAT at a large table, sifting through boxes of records. Occasionally, he would sneeze, and a soft voice from a few aisles over would bless him. Many of the records were not typed but, instead, handwritten in a crabbed fashion precluding comprehension. The thought of anyone in the future possibly needing the records of who married whom on what date was not what the office drone had been paid enough to even think about.

"I don't think I want to become a cop," the Squirt groused as he lifted one set of records out of the box he had just put a large stack into.

The voice had moved and now seemed to come from a much higher level in the stacks of large shelves filled with boxes. "Why not?"

The Squirt looked at the top sheet in the file. The handwriting was in pink ink and could be ancient Greek, Russian, or some form of Middle Eastern northern Arabic. He groaned and leaned back in the chair. "Because I'd rather track down all of these moron clerks and just shoot them. In 1868, three guys by the names of Sholes, Glidden, and Soule in Milwaukee, Wisconsin, built the first commercially viable typewriter. The S&G was manufactured by the sewing machine division of Remington's small arms. By 1880, the typewriter was changed by Remington, and the QWERTY keyboard with uppercase and lowercase was introduced, and the rest is history. So by the time these office idiots got their first job, the typewriter was already an office fixture..."

The young blonde in a white blouse that did nothing to hide her prodigious breasts rounded the shelves. Her glasses were shoved up into the great soft clumping of hair wound loosely onto the top of her head.

The Squirt finished, "So why the dingbats can't type the information onto the forms is beyond me or any reasonable explanation."

The blonde leaned against the towering shelf clutching a large file below her breasts. She studied the young man.

The Squirt squirmed. "What?" He blinked as he ran his hand over his head in case he had a cowlick standing up.

"How do you do that?"

"I licked my palm and just rubbed... oh, you didn't mean..." The Squirt blushed.

She smiled as her eyes lowered in a new evaluation. "No. No, I wasn't talking about your hair... and it's fine, by the way. I was talking about knowing about the typewriter."

The Squirt blushed even harder. His face dipped. "I wrote a paper on it last month."

"On typewriters? What kind of paper?"

"Regular typing paper—twenty-pound bond, soft-faced cellulose."

"No, not the paper, but the paper..." She suddenly realized he was teasing her, and it was her turn to blush. "I meant, what was the paper on and what was it for? I thought you said you didn't start at the academy until January."

"You might say I'm getting privately schooled in preparation for the academy." Thinking about Hooker and how his assignments still hadn't stopped, he groaned a little inside. "And, it might continue after, as well."

"So what was the paper on, if not the history of typewriters?"

"Actually, the history was for extra credit. But the paper was about filling out police reports dating back to the fifteenth century."

The blonde held up a large file and blew across the top, sending a cloud of dust into the air. "I think some of these files have been sitting here since the fifteenth century." She turned back to the young man. "So this *was* for the academy —police stuff?"

The Squirt leaned back in the chair. "Just as much as this investigation is police business." He rocked forward and stretched. It had been a long day chasing names through forests of bad handwriting, valleys of misfiled paperwork, and mountains of just paper forms useless to the search. "There is an old... well, older librarian who is kind of private tutoring me."

"What subject?"

The Squirt considered the young clerk. She had been the only clerk to want to assist in anything but sitting at their desk and doing as little as possible. In the Squirt's opinion, the county payroll was largely padded by large padded rear-ends that should be ejected. The exception was the blonde in front of him, Beth.

What had started with the Squirt waiting an hour at the counter for an answer, had become an invitation into the back stacks, and eventually, where they were now—the basement. Here was where the older records lay forgotten. Large cubes of paperwork sat in cardboard sarcophagi entombed in the catacombs of the county's heart and soul of dust and deterioration. But in the dead garden of the basement, there was a single spring daffodil.

The Squirt shook his head slightly, realizing he had been staring and was lost in the powder blue eyes floating above the full red lips. "I'm sorry, I was... um, and what did you ask?"

A slow smile tugged at the one side of her face. "I asked where you were taking me to dinner tonight."

The Squirt reran his trusted mental tapes. He was certain it had not been a question, but it was better than explaining the lack of a high school diploma. "How about a little Italian deli?"

She smiled. "Chiaramonte's? Sure, any day."

The Squirt looked around for a clock. Beth giggled. "We have an hour until I'm officially off." She pushed off the shelves. "I found these—and they are typed." She laid them on the end of the table. The stack was only four inches of very thin folders.

Pulling through the stack, she continued to explain. "These were misfiled for some reason. These are addendum reports for city or county employee's requests on cross transfers, and some of it is requests for special time off."

"What is special time off?"

"Having babies, death in the family, getting married, extended illnesses—stuff like that. Kind of like getting shot full of dime-sized holes." She smiled at the story he had told her earlier. After all, who is going to believe a guy could get shot full of holes the size of a dime—and still live?

"The holes were made by dimes, so think more like a slot, not a round." He held her eyes as he raised the side of his shirt. The large welts of surgical scar were still livid pink.

Her mouth dropped open and then closed as if it were holding a dime. Her eyes grew large as the red swelled up out of her blouse to her face. "I thought you were just bullshitting me to try to get in my pants..."

He dropped the edge of his t-shirt. "Why would I lie to get into your pants? They probably wouldn't fit me anyway." He sat stoic and only blinked once. Stella and Manny would be proud of him playing the deadpan face game. He enjoyed watching the young clerk become more and more flustered. For once, he wasn't the one on the end of a skewer.

He reached over and took a part of the stack. "Was this all of it, or was there more?"

Her mind had trouble shifting gears, but finally, the connection hit. "No, I mean... Yes, this is all of it. That's what made it stand out. It's not even in the right area. Some of these dates are only, umm... sixteen years old, and so they should still be upstairs in the county general area." She looked up at the Squirt. "And there should be a couple of boxes for each year." She pointed to the now two small stacks. "This is all there was—just sitting there in an unmarked box..."

The Squirt finished her thought. "Like someone had moved them here to hide them?"

"Exactly."

Johnny smiled, not feeling so much like the Squirt here. "Well, pull up a chair, partner, and let's see if we can figure out who is trying to hide what."

Much later, Beth yawned as she pushed the take-out boxes down the table. She blinked to clear her eyes and marveled as she watched the young man. She couldn't figure out which name she preferred. Johnny had an appeal, but the Squirt was a derogatory term she had heard the cops use, and Johnny owned it as an earned title. The man was a walking conundrum. His formal schooling had stopped midway through his freshman year of high school, but his love of reading, combined with his eidetic memory, pushed his learning and knowledge far beyond her two years at Santa Clara Junior College.

She leaned forward as she adjusted her glasses. Rereading the request for marital leave by an assistant district attorney, she thought it a bit quaint. The newlyweds were going to spend time in New York and visit Niagara Falls. Time requested—three weeks. She put the form on the done pile and moved to the next form.

A request for leave to give birth was accompanied by

two doctors' letters describing stressful conditions requiring bed rest for the last trimester.

A request for a sabbatical leave of three years to do missionary work in Bolivia as supported by the minister and three lay ministers' letters.

The request for emergency compassionate leave was accompanied by a telegram to *'cum now—she ded.'*

Beth leaned in close and read the next request for two-week marital leave. She read it again. The names fit, as did the date. She looked up.

She cleared her throat.

The Squirt looked up. His eyes cleared. He, too, was wearing out looking through all of the forms.

Beth leaned back. "Where would you go on your honeymoon?"

He frowned. "What?"

"You heard me." She leaned forward and crossed her arms on the table and forms. "Let's say we're getting married."

"When?"

She glanced down at the form and looked back. "December twentieth."

"Hawaii, if we could afford it. At least take the train down to sunny San Diego. Where would you?"

"If money was tight—San Diego or Mexico. But if I could have my fantasy—Tahiti."

The Squirt nodded. "Those work. But what about if it was the summer?"

"Are you asking me to marry you?" She giggled. "You haven't even asked me out on a date."

Johnny smirked and pointed at the take-out containers from Chiaramontes. "I took you to one of the most exclusive places to eat in the whole South Bay Area."

They both laughed, and the connection was complete. Any future date was a given.

Beth held up the form. "This is a request for two weeks to get married and honeymoon in... wait for it... none other than sunny San Francisco."

"Who is requesting it?"

"Deputy district attorney. My question is... who the hell would spend two weeks in San Francisco over Christmas and New Year?"

"Who is the blushing bride?"

"Who said anything about blushing?"

"Because you are... and your respiration is up, too. So she is...?"

"Dani—with an 'i,'" She spun the form over to him.

He read the form, and his smile grew. He looked up. "Do you know what this means?"

Beth nodded. "More than you know—it means we're on the wrong floor, the wrong building, and looking in the wrong direction." She looked at her watch. "But if we hurry, we can maybe get some work in before the library closes."

"Library?" He watched her stand as he pushed out his chair.

"Did I mention the word *hurry*?"

The librarian stepped into the small research room. "Beth, we're going to close in ten more minutes."

The hand waved over the microfilm machines. "Thanks, Marianne, we won't be much longer."

The Squirt's head was resting on her shoulder as she moved expertly through the microfilm. The images slid past with only brief moments of hesitation. They now knew who they were looking for and who they had become in the last sixteen years. What they now looked for was recent confirmation of one other thing.

The Squirt's hand shot out. "There." He waved a finger at the screen. "No, go back. More... more... there!" He leaned in squinting. "Can you make it..."

She expanded the view. The Squirt leaned back as the large shoulders and deep plunging V-necked dress adorned by a necklace and a large pendent swelled to fill the viewer.

Beth breathed. "Wow."

Johnny smirked. "Wow is right. I'll get you one as a wedding present."

They looked at each other.

He cleared his throat after a moment. "You asked why they would go only fifty miles away for their honeymoon—it was because it was familiar." They looked back at the picture of the couple at a gala event. "My guess is when he has to travel for his work, she doesn't go with him. Maybe fear of flying, but also maybe just uncomfortable with new surroundings."

Beth put her hand on the screen near the pendant. Her voice was soft and almost breathless. "If you're not kidding about the necklace, we can skip right to the third date."

CHAPTER TWENTY-ONE

THE DRIVE UP to Mendocino had been a smooth run. About Santa Rosa, Hooker had glanced over to see Candy nodding off, so he told her to climb into the sleeper. He slipped the eight-track of the Texas Boys Choir into the player and turned it up to just above low.

After a bit, Box thought it might be safe to go get a close look at the new person—and climbed up into the sleeper. Hooker glanced back as Box figured she might smell enough like the Squirt and settled in.

The next time Hooker looked back, Candy's arm was wrapped over the cat, and they were both either purring or dead to the world. Hooker just shook his head. There was just no figuring out his partner. The cat goes from only Hooker and Dolly can touch him to everybody skate in one brief summer. Hooker downshifted as he came into the town of Willets. *Next thing we know, Box is going to give up beating up every dog he sees.*

Hooker checked his mirrors to see how the Peterbilt was doing. *Nah, he'll never give up ripping a dog a new asshole—it's payback and too much fun for him.*

Hooker started thinking Box's love of fighting wasn't controllable—it was his nature. It was what he was used to. So if that goes for a cat that is almost human in certain ways, how much stronger would the comfort of a routine be for a human? Specifically—one Teresa Pappas—how far would she stray from what she knew?

Hooker mulled the question over until long after he had turned south in Fort Bragg. Candy had woken up, and Box shook himself as if he had never been touched by the stranger and took up a position on the dashboard to let Hooker know he needed some lawn.

Candy slid down into the passenger seat and looked about. "What did I miss?"

Hooker laughed as he saw a turn out close to some lawn. He looked over at the still sleepy-eyed Candy and teased, "Just a few herds of deer, a couple of elk, and a UFO."

Candy looked at him dully and smacked her lips and then rolled her head back in a zombie roll. Hooker groaned inside. *Oh, god, she is spending way too much time with Stella.* The zombie was the family response to stupid comments or questions.

"You must think I'm some kind of stupid, Hooker."

Hooker set the brakes and kicked his door open for the orange rocket. Sliding out of the conversation and truck was his only defense. He took it. Candy got out and stretched as she watched the strange thumping routine of checking the tires. Hooker checked the tires on the towed truck, too.

As Hooker and Box finished at the same time, they resumed their route west to the coast, and then south toward Mendocino. Candy watched as the sparsely wooded scenery turned to an ocean view. Hooker could tell she was working up to asking about something.

"Why do you do that?"

"What?"

"The big hammer on the tires." She turned in her seat toward Hooker.

"When the air pressure is correct, the hammer bounces just right in my hand. If it's too high, the hammer feels wrong on the strike. It's like hitting metal. If the pressure is low, the hammer won't bounce."

"But if you were getting a flat, wouldn't you know it?"

"Not really. Especially if it's one of the inside drivers— they can go flat and then shred, and you might never feel a thing. Meanwhile, you are throwing twenty-pound chunks of hard rubber out behind you. Those chunks can punch out a windshield and take a person's head clean off."

"You're kidding me."

Hooker looked over at her. His eyes were flat and lifeless.

"Oh, lord... you've seen it, haven't you?"

Hooker just nodded.

Candy sat back around quietly. She needed to process the new information. Hooker's hand dangled down and found the fuzzy ear. It wasn't clear to Hooker, who was more reassured by the rubbing of Box's ear, but he did know

Box purred, and he felt calmer. It was a symbiotic partner-ship, and every time Hooker rubbed the single ear left, a part of him remembered finding the tiny bloody handful of fluff in a cardboard box stuck under an abandoned car Hooker was to tow. The chewed up thing had mewed only once, and then settled into Hooker's coat and purred all the way to the vet's office. The vet had advised euthanasia for the dog-mauled kitten, but Hooker had turned his pockets out, and emptied his wallet on the table, stating he would get more—just save the cat.

A week later, he picked up the kitten in a box. But the cat preferred being inside his leather jacket, next to the beating of Hooker's heart and the smell of the starched white t-shirt. As he grew, the box was his home in the truck and had become his name.

"She's not your real sister..."

Hooker's mind shifted. He smiled slightly as he knew this was the real thing on Candy's mind. He gently shook his head no. He glanced at the directions on the clipboard and downshifted as he flicked his left blinker.

Moving the train of two trucks into the center turn lane, he answered the next question. "I was four when we first met, and she was six."

"Where?"

"I think we were somewhere south of San Bernardino— maybe Temecula area. It was a nice couple, and they had a couple of kids of their own but were older, like ten or twelve."

"When did you start considering her to be your sister?"

"I was about six when we were moved back down the

hill from a farm in Mentone. The older couple had never had kids, and they were going to try fostering. The place was in Riverside." Hooker slowed and eased off the street into a large parking lot. The signage matched up to the paperwork.

"I'll be right back." He grabbed the clipboard and slipped out of the cab. Candy watched him stride across to the building. She had never really watched him walk since being shot up. She smiled. He swaggered like Gary Cooper in High Noon.

A half-hour later, they were wheeling out of the yard. "Ready for some lunch?"

Candy kneaded the large lap full of purring orange fur. "Box and I want to know if there is a wharf with fresh crabs and lobster here too, like down in Monterey." She gave Hooker a large hungry smile. Box just looked at him with a half-closed eye.

Holding up directions. "If these are correct, I think we will be close."

The picnic bench on the lawn overlooking the ocean was its own delight. The food, on the other hand, was too much, too good, and beyond the hype by the trucking company's secretary.

Hooker leaned back and rolled his eyes. "Oh, boy, I think I need a nap."

Candy nodded down past the table at a section of the lawn. Box was stretched out sound asleep in the afternoon sun. Hooker nodded and got up to retrieve the moving blanket from the truck. The afternoon sunshine sounded better than the stagnant air in the sleeper of the truck.

Hooker spent his life in the truck, so even though the fall temperature wasn't warm, a light blanket over them made for a nice nap before heading south again.

"RIVERSIDE." CANDY REMINDED Hooker where he had left off.

"Riverside." Hooker's mind spun back. "I think I fell in love with her in a pile of leaves. The couple we were with... were nice. It was the last good home. They were older, but it was still fun. They understood or wanted to understand kids in a pile of leaves. The man raked all of the leaves from the two large yards and put them in a pile in the back yard for us to play in.

"Sissy was wearing a gray sweater—probably too large for her, but then, everything was the wrong size for any of us fosters." Candy nodded—she knew.

"There was something about the softness of the sweater that matched her long hair and the way she touched. Even when we were wrestling in the leaves, she was soft and gentle. It was almost like it would hurt her if she was strong or brutal."

The dark highway miles of asphalt rolled under the truck as Hooker thought. Candy didn't push. She was involved with her own feelings and memories.

"We were rolling around in the leaves. The smells of fall were intense. People burned the leaves back then. But... then Sissy suddenly hugged me and kept holding me... She held me until I stopped squirming until I was calm. Then she whispered in my ear. She told me we would always be brother and sister, no matter whatever happened."

Hooker looked over at Candy. "I think that is when I knew I loved her. I didn't understand love... heck, I'm not sure I do even now... but I cared more about her than I did about anything else."

Candy started to speak and then cleared her throat. "Forever love." She nodded and laid her head against the window and looked out into the night. Hooker smiled sadly and echoed the words in his mind. *Forever love.*

Hooker saw the Steele Avenue exit was two miles ahead. It was a major street he had taken several times before. He knew of a Thrifty drug store about a half-mile west of the highway. It was a bit out of his way, but it was just one of those kinds of nights. He glanced over at Candy. "If I stop, do you promise not to laugh or make fun?"

She looked over and frowned. "Why would I make fun?"

"I'm just saying..."

An hour later, when they got to the Apple Farm and Hooker opened his mouth to say hello, his sister laughed. "You two stopped for French vanilla ice cream, triple scoops in a sugar cone." She looked at Candy. "Oh, tell me he hasn't got you doing it, too."

Candy laughed as she raised her cold leather-jacketed arms and hugged Sissy. "Of course not, silly... I'm a waffle cone kind of girl." Her voice had the same thick huskiness from eating ice cream while riding with the windows down —a Hooker habit. The two just giggled.

"You sound just like my brother."

CHAPTER TWENTY-TWO

HOOKER SNICKERED LIKE a small child. The four chairs with their backs turned toward him, and his sister towered over them. They sat between the chairs, with blankets completing the canopy. Hooker's smile mirrored the goofy smile of his sister. Neither had ever thought they would be in a blanket tent ever again, not since the second home they had been moved to in Bakersfield.

"You sound like a little boy."

Hooker laughed. "I *feel* like a little boy."

Sissy smiled softly—almost sadly. "I thought this would be the best way for us to get back to talking... just us."

Hooker knew what she was trying to say. She wanted to wipe out the years of her being the Mouse—commander or queen of a large tribe of night people, the kind creeping about the dark crevices and cracks of society. She wanted to go back to before the owners of the foster homes had turned from caring people to predatory abusers and pedophiles. To reset the clock to when they didn't have to live in fear—when they were just happy children. Or at least as happy as a couple of orphans could be as they were moved from one house to another, sometimes more than twice in a year.

Hooker's face drew back on the right side, and he cocked his head over to the left as he watched his sister. "Remember the blue quilt?"

Her eyes lit up. She pursed her lips in thought—and then a guarded smile as her eyes softened. "Maude and JT Peltson."

"Pellerson." Hooker smiled as they remembered.

"It was made from her grandmother's dresses. I never knew if she was saying her grandmother was crazy, or the pattern of the quilt was crazy." They both snorted.

"They were the first black people I remember having seen. When we first got there, I kept waiting for them to wash the color off. It never did. I think she was the only one who ever sat me on her lap and just rocked me and hummed to comfort me."

Hooker nodded. "I saw you one night when I was supposed to be in bed asleep. Something had happened at school or something. You had been crying most of the afternoon."

Sissy was silent as she picked at her bare feet. She would just pick one up an inch and let it fall. Hooker knew she was thinking.

Sissy looked up and threw her hair behind her shoulder. "Remember the peach orchard across the road?" Hooker nodded with a small smile. "Those were some big peaches."

Hooker chuckled. "They probably tasted a lot better once they were ripe."

"Oh, you were sick as a dog." She pushed at his legs laughing... and then became very quiet.

"Dog?"

She nodded.

"He loved you with all his being, Sissy. He gave his life to save yours. He knew he would, I think, before the night."

She looked up at her brother.

"I think the night I was showing you how the killing would happen—he already knew and had been planning. For him, there was no plan B. It was all about saving you—killing Raven was just a bonus."

"It doesn't hurt any less."

"I hope it never does. He was special, so very special to you. I hope you have him in your heart all of your life. To love someone that deep—to be loved that much—is something most people don't even get to think about, much less know."

She picked up her foot and let it fall. "It's a two-edged sword."

"Yes."

Sissy watched his eyes. "Tell me about Willie."

Hooker looked out the side of his shaded eyes as he smirked. "What do you want to know?"

She giggled. "I already know about the dresses. The summer you and all of those Navy men built the big barn garage, I lived some of the time on the hill behind. I would watch from the shade of the chaparral. God, it was hot that summer."

Hooker snorted. "It's why those guys worked so slowly. There was beer and the pool at the end of the afternoon. I don't know who paid for all of the steaks, but I never ate so much meat."

"In the middle of the night, I used to come down and swim. The pool was cool."

"Willie's boyfriend at the time, Danny, had insomnia. He kept saying there was a water sprite who came out of the mountain to play in the water every night. We just thought he was nipping a little too much of Maddie's moonshine."

"He was the blond who was dying."

Hooker frowned. "How could you have known? He didn't know he had cancer until that winter."

Sissy shrugged. "He came out one night. He just stood on the patio—never said a word. He just watched. I'm pretty sure I was glowing pretty bright that night. He didn't know what to make of me. After a few minutes, he just turned and walked back inside. I never saw him again. But I knew then he was dying. I think he knew it, too."

Hooker thought about the yelling matches. Everything changed that winter. As it got bad, Hooker had decamped and bunked in at Manny and Stella's house. It had been a split living arrangement ever since. It was only in the last few years Hooker allowed himself to have more than a couple of extra T-shirts and jeans at Hacienda Romero.

The deciding factor had been the day Manny had a large dog door installed in the wall of the sunroom for Box to come and go as he wanted. Hooker had figured if they were going to make that much accommodation for a cat, then he might as well relax and be part of the family.

Besides, Stella was better at ironing his white T-shirts than he or Willie was.

"You're thinking about Willie?"

Hooker duck-lipped as he shook his head slightly. "Not just Willie—Manny and Stella, too... Well, actually, all of it." He looked up.

Sissy could sense where his mind was. She reached out and stroked her hand down along his cheek. "Don't. Please. I have no regrets. I chose my life. It was the one I was comfortable with. You were offered another path."

Hooker had many years to understand this truth. He snorted. "Offered! Hell, he smacked me on the butt with his newspaper. And then forced me to go have lunch with him." Hooker lay the back of his hand against his forehead.

Sissy laughed. She could tell Hooker loved the man he called his uncle and had fun talking about him. There was just a twinge of jealousy to have the kind of relationship they had. "So—tell me about those ugly dresses..."

CHAPTER TWENTY-THREE

ORMAN AND HOOKER sat in the late morning sun. The Adirondack chairs were perpetual icons on the sloping south-facing lawn. The fall mist hung in wisps through the bare black limbs of the orchard. The two men were bundled in large wool overcoats and Elmer Fudd hats. As Hooker sipped on the large steaming mug of coffee, he laughed at how he must look. Norman looked the part of a farmer, but Hooker felt the sham and the warmth of the costume. He had drawn the line at the large fuzzy gloves and settled for a pair of leather work gloves out of the truck.

After about twenty minutes, Claire Osofsky, knowing her husband, had brought out two large horse-hair sleigh blankets and spread them over the men's legs. She had topped off their mugs of coffee and returned to the warmth of the kitchen to prepare the soup for lunch.

Hooker realized this conversation would not be the

friendly pat on the family member's hand, telling them everything is fine. Sissy was anything but fine.

"Her skin seems to have cleared up."

The older physician and psychiatrist smiled wanly. "Yes, the extreme eczema has responded to the topical steroids. But the worry is—what is a maintenance dose for something this extreme? As for the phosphor imbalance, the steroid cream helps with the itching, so the lesions from the scratching have healed—but we have been unable to control the over productions of the phosphors, so she still glows in the dark. I'm afraid it's a genetic thing she will always suffer from."

Hooker took a sip of coffee as he thought about when his sister had started glowing. The home was on the outskirts of Bakersfield near some cotton fields. Down the road where they had better access to water, the melon fields started. Hooker had thought things might be better here. The beatings at the previous house had started to be more about having him naked than just a form of punishment. At least at the new house, there were no beatings. But there also was no door on the bathroom, and both adults would watch as the children as they used the toilet or bathed.

One night, Sissy had come to Hooker's bed. She told him to get under the covers where it was totally dark... except, this night, it was not. Sissy was giving off a soft glow. Years later, she used the glow to her advantage as the mystical witch to control her tribe of denizens of the night.

"What about... well, Sissy herself?"

"Mentally?" Hooker nodded. Norman rolled his lips—this was the tough question. "She will always be in some kind of care. At best, she might migrate into a restricted group home." Norman watched the shadows race across Hooker's face. "But, based on what you two grew up with, I would say eventually, she would be a better candidate for some kind of institution—if she lives that long."

"But she's not dying..." Hooker understood the delicate nature of the discussion.

"No, no, she's not dying—per se, but she and her organs and systems are frail. Think of her as 'a woman in her late eighties,' and you have some idea just how far removed she is from her actual age of twenty-seven. Physically, she will never get better than about eighty."

"Claire and I have always eaten a healthy diet. But now with your sister Claire here, we watch everything. In a way, it can be a strain, but we have come to find having her here as a blessing we never thought we would have."

Hooker smiled. This was an old refrain for him. "She's like the daughter you always wanted, but never even hoped to have."

Norman looked over with large eyes.

Hooker smiled. "I've heard it dozens of times from Stella, Dolly, and my Uncle Willie. Some families are just meant to be, and if it means they happen instead of being created, they are no less a family. I know I'm blessed with a large family who cares about me—and even without having ever met Sissy, they were willing to go to extremes to save her life."

Norman looked out across the orchards and thought about how true and powerful it all was. The animal nature to bond and become a collective is strong in some. He thought about his favorite time of the year when the large white boxes appeared in his orchards. He and Claire would lie on the fertile ground under the trees and listen to the masses of bees hard at work above them. It was the collective that was about the renewal of life.

"I know you said you would be coming down this year with Claire for Manny and Stella's wedding anniversary, but what about Sissy?"

Manny and Stella had gotten married on the quay in front of the troopship before he shipped out. When he kissed his bride, four thousand soldiers whooped, whistled, and clapped. Ten minutes later, Manny had walked up the gangplank headed for Korea.

Stella and Claire had stood on the quay and watched the ship until it made a left turn toward the Golden Gate Bridge. Then they had bribed a sailor to take them across in the water ferry to San Francisco's tenderloin district where they danced until dawn at the USO, celebrating the marriage. With the sun coming up, they had taken an officer up on his offer to drive them the long way back around the bay to Oakland. It was Christmas morning. Every year after, Claire came to visit. She and Stella would get dressed to the nines and then go dancing in San Francisco—without Manny. It was tradition.

Norman stirred and looked over at Hooker. "You were saying... oh, yes, your sister. We've made arrangements for her to stay with someone. It will be fine. She'll be in loving hands." The man smiled reassuringly.

. . .

FRIDAY MORNING CAME TOO FAST for Hooker, as it did for the two new sisters who stood hugging in the front hall. Hooker's heart warmed from how Sissy and Candy had bonded from the start. They both recognized they were the flipsides of the same coin. Candy hadn't known anything about Sissy but had dealt with the creatures of the night. Sissy had been the matriarch of those creatures and had known a lot about the waitress, who had looked after the extended members of her tribe. Deep down, Sissy would say it was their fate to become close bonded. Hooker was just happy to be the center of the bonding.

He cleared his throat. "Do you two need to get a room? There is fuel burning, and Mae is getting overheated."

Sissy looked at Candy and then at her brother. "Someone else is getting overheated as well." Candy giggled into Sissy's neck and then pulled away.

"Okay, mister... rip me away from my sister. Drag me back down to the hell of books and classes. I'll just probably starve away from Claire's fine food as well."

Claire and Norman laughed. "Oh, I highly doubt Stella will let you starve. She taught me everything I know about cooking." She hugged Candy and then gave way for Norman.

Norman, ever the practical one, hugged her and let go. "It's only a few weeks until Christmas, so you won't starve too much before Claire and I come down."

Candy turned toward Sissy. "I wish you could come, too." She put her hand out, and the woman took it delicately.

"Arrangements have been made. You'll be fine. You

need to study, but we'll see each other again soon enough." They hugged again.

Hooker knew his sister, and he smelled a bit of over-acting going on, but time was wasting, and they would have to backtrack out to the 101 to pick up the return tow. He had opened the door before there was any more hugging or sentiments.

Later, as Hooker checked the mirrors to see how the towed bus was doing, he took in the pensive look on Candy's face as she studied her textbook. "Why the serious face?"

Candy looked up with a washed-out frown. "What?"

"You're even chewing on the right side of your lower lip."

She felt the lip with her tongue. She shrugged. "I was just thinking about Sissy." Candy loosened her belt and turned in the seat. "For the last ten years of her life, she was totally free, no constraints. But now, she will always have to live with someone."

Hooker weighed the concept. "Are you free? You have no rent to make, no food bill, not even a car payment or insurance payment. So you don't have any bills, you just have to go to school merrily.

"But there is an underlying responsibility. It's not written or spoken, but it's there.

"And, it was the same with her. No, they didn't have any responsibilities or obligations of society as we know it—but she was far from free. Dog was free, most of the others were free—but she was trapped in a prison of her own doing."

"Because she was the queen, she was responsible for all of them." Candy turned and looked forward down the road. "So do you think she is free now?"

Hooker curled his lips. "No, you clearly see the future for her. She will always be dependent on someone. But she is happier now without that life and death responsibility every single minute of every day. I think it was Shakespeare who said something about 'a weary head who wears the weight of a crown.'" Hooker checked the mirrors and upshifted.

"Oh, my sweet prince, now you willst speak to me of the bard of Stratford-on-Avon?" Candy giggled. "And here I thought you were just a pretty knight in a shiny steed."

Hooker chuckled.

Candy's smile faded. "But, seriously, you think she's going to be okay? I mean long term."

Hooker glanced over at the serious face but smiled at the freckles and ponytail. "How comfortable are you with the apartment, the car, and Stella and Manny taking you and your brother in?"

Candy thought quietly. "It's still uncomfortable."

"Enough to walk away uncomfortable? Enough to move back out and give up nursing school—that uncomfortable?"

"No. But you know what I mean. It's weird. You know how we grew up..."

"Yes. You two grew up the same as Sissy and me. Sissy and I—you and the Squirt, two makes of the same movie. And that is why I understand.

"Other people just used us, beat us, shit on us, and that's what we came to expect from the world. And then along comes Uncle Willie, who slaps me on the butt and then takes me home. Not to his bed—but gives me my own bed. He bought me clothes, and fed me, and asked for nothing in return. The return was something I had to figure out when I really understood he wanted nothing from me but my wellbeing. Then when the shit hit the fan with his boyfriend at the time, Stella and Manny showed me another bed was waiting. It was unconditional. All I had to do was learn to accept it and just say thank you.

"The night I met Stella, Claire, and Manny was a Christmas eve. I had cocoa and fresh chocolate chip cookies. I took the tow and hauled the girls up to Palo Alto to drop off Stella's Caddie at the dealer, and then took them home. By the time we got down to the hacienda, it was almost dawn. Manny knew I wouldn't take payment for the tow or accept a tip. Dolly had warned him. So he told me I couldn't refuse a Christmas present Stella had gotten me the year before, and he had just been holding on to it for me."

Hooker glanced over. "You know my money clip."

"With the little knife in it? Sure."

"Christmas morning, Manny gave me the clip with a few bills in it. The one showing was a five. I started to remove the bills to give them back. Manny told me a gentleman never counts the money in front of the person giving him a gift. In the evening, I went to pay for dinner—there were two hundred-dollar bills wrapped by the five."

Candy leaned back. "Whoa."

"Yeah, it was huge then. But a few years later, I understood it was just one of the little things. It's not the T-shirts hanging in the closet—it's that Stella washes and then irons them with just the right amount of starch. It's not the food on the table. It was when I dragged home a cat who didn't like anyone else. Stella still always buys food for Box, too. Maybe someday Box will understand and warm up to her. But it doesn't matter to Stella. Box is part of me, and it's enough for her. You and the Squirt were part of me, and it was enough for them. But you two have become more than that. You are also becoming the children they have always wanted but could never have. But with you, Stella doesn't have to share you with Willie. So she gets the daughter all to herself. And if it means I hang around a bit more, she's happy there, too."

"So with Sissy?"

"She's where you are. She trusts me. And, she is starting to trust Claire and Norman will take care of her and love her like a daughter... it just takes time for it all to soak in."

"Are we talking about Sissy or me?"

"All three of you... heck, even me. It's been ten years, and I still have to pinch myself to know this is real. This truck is in my name. The company is in my name. Willie is just a co-signer on everything. The two beds are mine. I don't know if you noticed, but there are only three keys on this ring. One is for Mae, one is for the lockbox on the back, and the other key is to both houses. Willie had them all keyed alike so I could come and go at will."

"And with all the freedom..."

"I'm still not free. Even a bird has to find a worm every day."

Candy mulled it all over as she watched the highway.

Through the trees, she could see the twinkling of lights across the bay to San Francisco. She thought about finding herself a worm...

She turned. "Speaking of finding things... did you ask Sissy?"

"About the waitress, Dani? Yeah—she gave me the name of a woman who might help if the Squirt hasn't solved the problem first. You know, it was amazing how really connected throughout the South Bay Sissy was. She knew about things down in Santa Cruz and up around the San Francisco airport. Her network was a lot more extensive than I had ever imagined."

Candy nodded. "She's a pretty amazing woman, too. Did you know she read over a hundred books a year?"

Hooker turned dumbfounded. "How? Where?"

"She had people bring them to her. She even had a library card... but never used it."

"What did she read?"

"A lot of best sellers serious stuff, but also, a lot of the classical stuff too."

"Like Shakespeare?"

"Some, she liked the dystopian nature of a lot of his works. It made her realize the things weren't just recently this way. But there was a lot of other stuff—more upbeat. Someone brought her the required reading list from Stanford, and it was just the start. She eventually got the lists from the nine colleges in the Bay Area. She said she had about nine books left to complete all of the lists. But Norman and Claire have their own lists—she has a lot of time to devote to reading."

"And here I was worried you two were just exchanging notes about me."

Candy laughed because she knew Hooker didn't have that kind of ego, just shy. "Oh, we did. She understands about you reading a lot about your truck and cars and stuff, but she thinks you should read some books like *Metropolis* and a newer one called *I, Robot*."

Candy looked to her right across the San Francisco Bay. The city was laid out like a carpet of Christmas tree lights. Her mind drifted. "Did you ever have a Christmas tree?"

Hooker thought. It was something he had never thought about or realized. The money clip in his pocket was the only gift he had ever gotten for the holiday. "No. And I had never thought about it. Manny and Stella were raised Jewish as well as Dolly. Dolly's holiday is New Year's Eve when she does up southern style ham hocks and black-eyed peas. In the south, it's all about good luck."

"But I thought Dolly was Stella's sister and Jewish? And weren't they raised in Montana or something? Where does the southern stuff come from—especially the ham?"

Hooker laughed. "I said *raised* Jewish, not practicing." He glanced over. If you talk to her much, she has a little southern twang in her speech, but where it came from is anybody's guess. But I do know that on New Year's Eve, most of the people there eating have the same twang, and they or their families are originally from Texas to the Carolinas."

"But no Christmas tree."

"No tree."

"What about Willie?"

"Bachelor—no need." Hooker glanced over. "What about you and the Squirt?"

"Never had one. Never thought about it before."

As they started across the Richmond Bridge, Candy realized where they were—or wasn't. "Why come all the way over here instead of going down the Golden Gate Bridge?"

"Not allowed to tow through the city. Those three miles could net me a two-hundred-dollar ticket."

"But you towed through the city going up."

"Had you ever been across the Golden Gate before?"

"No."

"It was worth the risk of a ticket to take you across. Besides, the cops in San Francisco at four in the morning are all over in the Tenderloin and Bay Front having dough-nuts. So the risk was almost not there. But right now, the city, especially the park, is crawling with cops."

"Oh." Candy watched the bridge end as she watched the lights on the bay. "So you did it for me."

"I thought you would like it."

"I did. I liked it very much... especially because I was with you."

Hooker chuckled softly. "Merry Christmas."

CHAPTER TWENTY-FOUR

THE RAIN POUNDED on the two rain slickers. The yellow had long been camouflaged with swipes of burn from hot mufflers and engines as well as smears of grease etched into the rubber. Cold hands worked the chains. The gloves had long been soaked from the December flood from the sky.

Hooker screamed into the storm at the yellow blob at the other end of the mangled tractor and trailer. The derailed train it had hit was someone else's problem. "Don't worry about the axle, its toast. Just wrap the chain around what is solid. We'll have to jerk this bastard off the rails before we can sort it out." Hooker knew he would have to split the tow. Everything about this mangled mess was screaming for a flat-bed trailer.

The Squirt backed out from under the trailer. "Jerk..."

The lightning was close enough that the crash of thunder was deafening. Hooker swore, but he knew what the Squirt had screamed. The levers in his hand were slipping, so he grabbed a rag and gripped them. Pulling them out actuated the system, pulling them up wound the cables in, and dragged the trailer around. Hooker watched the outrigger spuds. They swung out from the sides of the truck to stabilize and lift the rear tires up, so the truck became a twenty-two thousand-pound dead weight to pull from.

Even the thunder couldn't cover the scream of steel on steel as the trailer dragged off the railroad tracks. Hooker watched where the tractor had been punched into the trailer. He hoped for some movement to show them separating. They moved as one. The thunder covered Hooker's swearing. There would be no quarters dropped in the swearing jar tonight. The storm had Hooker's back.

As Hooker and the Squirt looked at the tractor half-buried in the trailer now sitting off the tracks, Hooker worked out the figures. "Jacked this way, the whole mess weighs over eighteen tons but is also almost thirty feet wide. I think we'll have to cut them apart." He looked over at the Squirt, who was leaning against the back of Mae West with his eyes closed.

Hooker was getting used to the look. The kid's mind worked in some strange but amazing ways. He was by no means the 'dumb kid' Hooker first took him for. "What are you thinking?"

"How much weight do you think a 'J' hook could take without straightening?" The kid was talking about the large hooks ubiquitous to towing. They looked like a fishing hook for catching whales and attached to twenty feet of heavy chain.

"A hell of a lot, if they are set right. I think the chain is rated for twenty or thirty tons. Why?"

The Squirt smiled evilly. "Let's tie off the front end of the tractor and the back axle of the trailer to the railroad rail. They will have to replace it after a derailment anyway." He pointed to the points and then indicated the middle. "Then we can hook into the cross-member of the tractor, right there before it disappears up into the trailer. If nothing else happens, at least we are trying to straighten the mess out."

Hooker grabbed the kid by the back of his neck through the hood of the slicker. "You sure you want to be just a dumb cop? You're good at this stuff."

The kid smiled shyly. "Let's see how it works out first."

The kid dragged out chains and hooks and set them as Hooker pulled in the outriggers. Jumping into the cab to relocate Mae for a better pull, Hooker grabbed the mic from behind his head.

"Mama?" He called over the shop radio going to Dolly's credenza.

"Go, Hooker."

"Could you please call Jose down in Gilroy and tell him we need both of his low-boy trailers. We're still working on the recovery, but these will have to be trailered."

"10-4, Hooker. I called him thirty minutes ago. The Chips called in for Tri-State to come down from Fremont, but they only have Mike and a standard. Their low-boys are on long-haul. And I figured you would want to work with the chorizo brothers anyway."

Hooker laughed at her nickname for the brothers who

made some of the best Mexican pork sausages in the South Bay. Hooker had never known the brothers to be raising less than a dozen hogs at any time, with six hogs worth of sausage and hams hanging in their cool room. If you want chorizo or prosciutto ham—you give the Gomez brothers some juicy tows.

"Thanks, mama. I'll watch for Jose and Lito."

The double click came as he hung the mic.

Once the ends were chained off, the Squirt set about binding the two tow cables to the two sides of the cross-member. Hooker watched. As the configuration became obvious, the dynamics of the 'pull' also became somewhat apparent to Hooker. Geometry was a word to Hooker, but he could tell it was something alive for the Squirt.

The Squirt finished and wiped his gloves on the slicker as if it might help his wet hands inside. He moved over to the side with the levers Hooker was holding. Hooker looked at the proud kid. "Do I pull them together or one at a time?"

The kid beamed—Hooker saw his plan. "Together to start, it will apply the pressure. Then once the join is strained, we can start working the strain."

Hooker thought about the idea. He wasn't going to steal any of the kid's thunder. Smiling, he stepped aside and offered his open palms at the controls.

There was a split second of hesitation as the kid grasped what had just happened. Suppressing his smile, he stepped over to the work. Hooker watched as the kid played the levers and winches with the finesse of a concert violinist. The join moved toward them, and then stopped. From the sound of the winches, they could tell there was strain working to free the tractor.

Hooker reached out and put his hand on the Squirt's two holding the levers. "Hold it a minute. Just leave them as they are. Let the strain work for us." Then Hooker grabbed the sleeve of the Squirt's slicker, and they walked away for about fifty feet and watched.

Hooker thought about watching the original paint job on Mae dry one day in August, so many years before. The clear coat lacquer, loaded with mother-of-pearl, had shot on foggy. Hooker had started swearing, but Willie's boyfriend at the time had just held up his hand to wait. As the clear coat had dried, the fog cleared, and the pearl appeared and then disappeared. It would only reappear under the right lighting. It was the magic of mother-of-pearl in the clear paint. The candy-apple paint of the blue was static and never changed. It was the pearl that gave the truck the look of changing like a living beast of the night as she slid past neon or fluorescent lights.

As they stood watching what appeared to be nothing happening, two large trucks with low-slung flatbeds drove up. The door of the lead truck opened, and a large Mexican American dropped to the ground then clambered back up into the cab. The other, almost as tall but fatter man, walked up in his bright orange slicker. "Lito hates wearing the rubbers. Some day he will become a daddy and learn."

Hooker's grin pulled sideways. "Hola, *jefe*. Glad you two were in town."

The man smiled. "Dolly, my angel, told me some

pendejo called for the *pienchy vatos* at Tri-State. I guess that Chip will never sit at a certain table, eh, *jefe?*"

Hooker shrugged along with an evil smile. "Some people never learn; some just never know."

The man laughed as he glanced back at what Hooker was looking at and who he really meant. His little brother was running over while he struggled to pull his slicker on.

Hooker couldn't let the chance pass to have some fun. "Lito, you might need to have your skanky sister show you how to pull a rubber on."

The kid laughed but still struggled, not realizing someone else had snapped the bottom two snaps. "Bite me, Hooker."

Jose looked down at the two snaps and smiled at Hooker, who had noticed them, too. It was an old practical joke, played in an area where the use of the jackets was a very rare occasion. "So what are we waiting for, *jefe?*"

"Waiting? We don't need no stinking waiting, Jose. We are working. Or, I should say, Mae is working. We are just supervising." Hooker smiled a large Hollywood toothy smile.

"But you are just..."

The creak and explosion came at the same time. The forty feet of run-out cable swam back toward and over the working deck and reached out for the four men.

"Jesus..." The two Mexican drivers dove into mud puddles. Hooker and the Squirt just slowly turned to look at the other two.

The Squirt, deadpan, offered, "They sure like getting all muddy."

Hooker finished the grinding. "They had a strict mother. No mud pies, no dirt. It had to come out some-time—one of those sad facts of life about them Gilroy kids."

The two muddy men harmonized, "Bite me, Hooker."

Hooker smiled lopsidedly as he turned to the kid and backhanded the Squirt's belly. "Let's go look at your handiwork."

The tractor had shifted almost six inches. With a couple of more set-ups, and pulls, the one mess became two objects they pulled and prodded up on to the two low-boy trailers. As the sun was just starting to peek over the eastern hills, the trucks were chained and ready to move. Hooker looked down the service road and could see a large crane standing by.

"*Jefe,* let me buy you both breakfast up on Monterey Highway. These bones are going in the back lot for the Fly, but Mike won't be there until eight to run the crane."

Jose leaned out of the window of his cab. "Coffee and omelets at Just Breakfast sound good to me. Lito will eat roadkill or even the asphalt, so we no have to ask him."

Hooker and the Squirt loaded into Mae, and they nosed out ahead.

"How hard is it to re-knit the loop on the broken cable?"

Hooker looked at the kid and smiled. "Don't worry about it. The cables are three years old, and this is just the right excuse for me to replace them. I should have pulled them last spring, but I was a little short on dimes." The two laughed at the dime joke. Each of them had enough dimes and bits to be a pair of two-bit characters.

Hooker snapped his fingers. "Before I forget, how did you do with your research?"

The kid smiled and leaned back. "My next research paper isn't due until mid-January. I even have photos of the wedding and some even more recent photos you'll find very interesting."

Hooker frowned. "Recent?"

"Last month, to be exact—she's in a nice dress, but the pendant necklace you will find even more interesting."

CHAPTER TWENTY-FIVE

S TELLA WALKED DOWN the hall. In the end, she knocked lightly on the door. A moment and the door cracked—the head of wild hair and blurry eyes appeared.

Stella passed through two hangers draped with a freshly ironed t-shirt and jeans. Light starch on the jean's creases, medium starch on the entire shirt. Just the way the Squirt liked it. Both being almost brand new did not escape the young man's eye.

Stella did not even pause to knock on the next door. She could hear the shower, and Box was at the door. She opened Hooker's bedroom door and let Box in. Stepping to the bathroom door, she hung the clothes on the hook.

"Breakfast is in twenty minutes, Hooker."

The response was garbled by the flood of water as he hit the valve turning on the six-head body flush for twenty seconds. Stella smiled. She remembered the first time

Hooker had hit the valve. The scream had Manny throw his mug in the air just as he was taking a sip at the dining table. She chuckled. Manny had really loved that mug shaped like the torso of a naked buxom gal. The lettering simply said, 'The Three Best Things.' In sympathy for his loss, Stella had a custom mug made. It was a large black mug with his gold detective shield on it. *Gotta love those powerful six-head shower blasts.*

Manny looked up as she returned from delivering her fresh ironing. "What are you laughing about now?'

"Manny Romero, if I divulged everything, your hair would turn white and start to curl." She ran her fingers over his short curly salt and pepper hair. "Oh, I see it's already taking effect."

She swung her hip out in a dance as his left backhand just missed spanking her britches.

"Should I load the boys up on pancakes?" She sauntered into the kitchen part of the large room—her domain and queen-dom.

Manny snapped the Mercury News and folded it into quarters. "I think your sister is going to stuff them with enough carbs. You might consider packing them down with more protein. It will calm Hooker down and keep the Squirt from pissing his pants tonight."

She looked over her shoulder and frowned.

"Not at Dolly's, but after."

She turned around, still frowning. "And why would..."

Manny rolled his head, and then could not complete the zombie—he started choking on his evil laugh. "Because

Candy invited four of the nursing students and three of them the Squirt was more John than Squirt with... if you catch my drift."

Stella started to laugh. "And we also extended an invitation to the new girl from the County Clerk's office..."

"Elizabeth."

"I think she goes by Beth."

The two were laughing low and evil when Hooker strolled in. Upon seeing them both doing the evil, no-good laugh, he peeled out his impersonation of Ricky Ricardo. "Lucy... you have some 'splainin' to do."

Breakfast was twenty minutes late.

Wednesday afternoons normally consisted of doing things that kept Hooker clean for Dolly's dinner at Dispatch at six o'clock sharp. Today was no exception.

Hooker and the Squirt walked through the Emergency Room of Valley Medical Center and straight to the elevators. The doors slid back at the fourth floor, and Hooker led the parade. They had to stop at three small restaurants to find someone who still had matches. Thankfully, Hooker remembered after leaving paperwork off at the Fly's that Chick-n-Ribs was right up around the corner and on the way to Valley Medical Center.

Five large women stood almost as a host as Hooker walked through the Billing Department's door with twenty-nine candles burning. "Okay, who's turning twenty-nine again this month?"

It was nobody's birthday, but it did keep Hooker on a lot of people's good side. Hooker counted on the statistic there were more fat necks to nuzzle in the billing office than any place in the hospital. Hooker knew how to be number one in their hearts and minds, if not their necks and giggles.

It also being Christmas Eve accounted for the second layer and extra frosting. There wasn't a single set of hips in the office who would ever tell him there was too much frosting.

At eight minutes before the strike of six, Hooker and the Squirt had made their Christmas rounds of deliveries, received checks, hugs, and seasoned kisses. It was a good night.

Hooker looked down the table. The table was perfect. Sitting on the left side of Hooker at the head were Micha and Bobby Sue. Sitting across were the mayor and his wife, Dani. Next pairing down the table was Ace across from the Squirt. Sitting next to the Squirt, and unsure why he was there, was the large Filipino, PD Officer James Aligo, who sat across from the Police Commissioner Paul.

Chet, a CHP captain, was still out of uniform, as he was still out on disability leave. Chet was sitting across from a blond-haired woman—who was a mystery to almost everyone but kept sneaking unsure glances at Chet. The table was finished at the end with not one but two people, as Uncle Willie and Maddie looked the quintessential outliers of the group. Hooker almost laughed when he first saw them and knew there had to be a story behind Maddie not only getting Willie into a suit, but also a tie. They looked like they were going to church somewhere in the Midwest.

With the food on the table, the soft-spoken niceties

were finished, and the cross-table, as well as down-table exchanges, began. This was the nature of this table, this night, this dinner. This is where the real power of Dolly began.

Hooker sipped on his coffee to clear his mouth and tried to hold his smile in check. Only two people were supposed to know the following information. At least—before the first week in January. "I understand the city is getting a new dog next month, Paul."

Hooker's timing was to perfection. His friend almost choked on his bite of bread. The entire table watched as the flustered commissioner struggled to swallow. Dolly was standing by and reached over with a healthy whack to the back. Her filling the blonde's coffee never wavered. Dolly was an expert at what she did—running her table.

Paul looked with watering eyes down the table at Hooker. He turned his head to frown at Dolly, who was now fussing over Maddie and Willie. She looked up and then spoke up. "Don't look at me in that tone of voice, young man. I have nothing to do with this. This was all Hooker."

Paul looked back to the head of the table. "Care to fill me in on how you know about such a closely guarded piece of information?"

Hooker leaned back, pulling the napkin across his lap. "All I can tell you is I was in Marin County and beyond this last month." He strained to ignore the Squirt, who he knew was pulling a perfect deadpan. Hooker could sense the kid was continuing to eat leisurely.

"But now that the dog is out of the bag, so to speak... you want to make nice with the new K-9 officer?"

Paul looked at the squinting eyes of the affable officer. James wiped his mouth. His voice was more of a deep rumble than words. "What did he say?"

Paul smiled. "He said, you're getting the dog you have wanted for several years."

James sat up with his body shaking from a quiet laugh. His smile dragged off to the right side as he looked down the table. "I'm getting a puppy for Christmas?"

Hooker laughed and nodded. Maddie started clapping. Most at the table had no idea how many times James had submitted his paperwork for K-9.

James turned back to Paul. "Do I get to take him back to King and Story, or do I have to move?"

"I thought it was the point of you wanting a dog—to clean up the Gun & Knife club?"

James nodded. "Part of it. But, mostly, I just wanted to get a good-looking partner finally."

The table enjoyed a good laugh and enjoyed the news.

The plates were wiped clean of dinner, and the last bits of coffee were sipped. Curiosity finally got the best of Hooker. Tradition at the table was no introductions made, and for the most part, none was needed. Tonight, Hooker knew half the diners were somewhat of a mystery. The conversations had been more about the season and how commercial things had become and less about the day-to-day struggles of jobs or family. Hooker kept waiting for some clue to the mystery woman, but none was forthcoming.

"Chet," Hooker began, "there is a mystery at this table... and you know how I hate an unsolved mystery..."

Chet looked at Dolly, who had stiffened and then relaxed. After all, it was Hooker doing the asking. Chet daubed at his lips, and then pulled the napkin into a rod and laid it beside his plate. He looked at his smiling dinner guest. "This is Doctor Sylvia Stowe. She is the county shrink." He looked up to Hooker. "She holds my career in her hands. She recently suggested the reason I am so stressed and have the headaches is that I have no friends. She thinks if I had a couple of friends, I might get out more often and enjoy life."

Hooker took a measure of the man to see if the twinkle in his eye was just about having fun or if maybe something might be a little bit more. He turned his head toward the psychiatrist. "I agree, I think Dolly, Willie, and I... heck even Micha and the Squirt have been telling him the same. He just hides away in the little house of his... cleaning his guns, polishing the pine wall paneling, shampooing the carpet, mowing the lawn, and looking out big window at the gophers in his lawn. Therefore, if you can get him to meet someone or at least get a dog like James here is doing, we would really appreciate it."

The woman smiled. "I think I underestimated Chet. He does seem to have quite the support network in place already. Nevertheless, it was good to see it in action tonight and to meet all of you. I think we can look at other reasons for the headaches... maybe while he is back on duty this next year."

Hooker jumped in before Chet. "Say... in January?"

She smiled. "I'd take your advice as a good plan and doable."

From the other room, a large belt of sleigh bells rang, and all conversation was over.

Karen called out from the dispatching wall of cords snaking into holes from other holes. "Listen up. Ace, you just caught a rollover on Capital and Snell. Hooker, Don is already on his way, so stand down. Ace, you are to swing by the shop and fetch the trainee and see if you two can handle things. If not, Don will help, but you get the full ticket. Merry Christmas.

"Micha, if you would be so kind as to take that, also. 3-4-7-Alpha has a couple of drunks parked creatively at the Chesboro cut-off.

"James, you have a party getting out of hand in the Almaden Valley. I have your paperwork here. Sorry you don't have your dog or a cute partner yet.

"Bobby Sue, as always, great to see you again, but you are needed to administer to the unwell.

"Merry Christmas to all and be careful out there."

She turned back to the large board, plugged another cord into another hole, and answered another call. The table rose as a ragged host. Hugs and handshakes were exchanged as Ace headed for the door with Micha close behind.

Hooker extended his hand to the mayor. "Sir, if you and your wife would please join me for a little bit in the office, I have something to talk to you about."

The mayor's wife started to say something in protest,

but the mayor squeezed her hand on his arm ever so slightly. "Of course, we will, Hooker. You have my interest piqued."

As they moved through the door, Hooker looked back at Willie and Maddie. Maddie nodded slightly as her eyes blinked gently. She confirmed the identity.

CHAPTER TWENTY-SIX

A s Hooker shuffled through a couple of papers on the top of the file, the couple did what sophisticated couples do when they aren't sure of the circumstance they are in—they fidgeted with only tiny movements. From the top of his vision, Hooker caught the slight movements.

"I'm sorry. I apologize for my seeming unpreparedness." Hooker looked up at Franklin Welton, the Mayor of San Jose, and his lovely wife, Danielle—*Please, call me Dani* Welton. Hooker evaluated the fidgeting. "You see, I don't want to waste your time, but I do want to make sure I tell this story to the best of my knowledge."

The mayor glanced out of the office window. In the dark of the larger area, he could see the top of Dolly's head working at her desk. For those in the know—the custom stainless-steel chair with its four hydraulic rams supported the weight of the chair, the person who sat in it and the power she wielded—the symbolism was not lost.

He looked back at Hooker—the man who had been sitting alone at the head of the dinner table that night. With a furtive glance, his eyes danced across the dark figure of Squirt, silently buried in the gloom of the darkest corner of the office. The mayor was hyper-aware that the young man had watched everything at the table, had listened intently to every conversation, and yet had said no more than a few words the entire time. He was as much of a mystery as this clandestine meeting was.

The mayor patted his wife's hand as he cleared his throat. "Take your time, Hooker. We have no other plans for tonight," the man lied.

Hooker put the papers back into their original order and placed them on the thick folder. He rested his hands on the whole. Taking in the couple for the umpteenth time, Hooker started.

"This story starts back about 1950 when a young girl debatably turned twenty-one and started work at a local roadhouse in the Salinas valley. The bar was on one of the unmarked back roads leading out to all of the truck farms. The road was a popular shortcut between Salinas and Hollister. The bar was simply named The Mail Pouch. Why waste money on a sign when one was already painted on the one end of what used to be a grain barn."

THE ROTTING SMELL of vegetation always got worse as the summer and crops moved into the high gear of scorching heat. The lettuce, cabbage, squash, and other crops ungleaned, lay in the fields yet to be disked back under as green manure.

The lanky figure stepped down from the driver's side of the truck. Danny Robinson swung the truck door shut with a rusty protest. The latch begrudgingly caught with a greasy thud. The 1936 stake-side truck had seen better days.

The passenger and friend, Hank Pappas, came around the nose of the battered truck. What had once been a green truck was showing more signs of red undercoat and brown rust. Hank pushed his finger at the large patch of soft metal held in place by only rust. "One of these days, this chunk of rust is going to let go and fly right into the fan. Then this old girl is going to explode or just die in your hands."

"Hank, you've been poking at the soft patch all summer, and it's still there. Probably be there when we are old and gray." Danny turned toward the roadhouse front door. "Now quit your pokin' at the rust, and let's see how your sister is working out tending bar."

Hank pulled his wide-brimmed Fedora from his head and beat at his clothes. The dust seemed to swell out around him, and then as he started walking, reassumed its place back on his clothes.

Danny held the door and teased his younger friend. "You know... they have this amazing place in town. It's called a Laundromat. You can get even those clothes clean."

The younger man stuck his middle finger up and mock picked his nose as he walked past and through the door. The dim of the interior felt cooler, but only as the shade from a shade tree feels cooler.

"Hey, y'all, where's my little sister?"

The rheumy-eyed man looked up from the end of the long bar, the sudden noise waking him more than any kind of intelligent response to a question he didn't understand in his stewed condition. His fingers were frozen around a half-finished tall shot glass.

The two younger men sat down at stools in the middle of the long counter. Hank tried again to stir some life in the old man. "Hey. Old man... Hey, where is the bartender?"

The dark-haired gal came out from the back with a case of beer easily carried under each arm. Her sleeves were rolled up like most field hands. Her strong arms and shoulders were standard on most of the young men in the valley who worked the fields. They showed she had never sought out anything less than working in the fields with the rest of her family.

Danny sat at the bar and admired the ease and grace the strength brought to the attractive wide face. As she bent to shove the cases on the lower shelf in the cooler, he leaned forward to judge the fit of her denim jeans.

Hank backhanded the older man's arm. "That's my sister you're ogling."

Danny blushed for just a second as he looked at his friend. "And a nice sister she is to ogle, too."

Teresa Pappas had smiled before she stood up. After spending a lifetime in the fields tending and picking crops, it was finally nice to have a girl's assets appreciated. Even if she did know, she could arm wrestle most of the field hands in the valley, and win.

She stuck her hands into the warm wash water and stood slowly drying them on a bar towel. She studied the lanky older man with her brother. She figured he was some-where between thirty-five and fifty, but age wasn't an issue with her. He had a certain lean, but strong look about him she found attractive.

Throwing the towel over her shoulder, she stepped over in front of the two men. "What can I get you two?"

By the third round of long necks, it hadn't surprised either Danny or Teresa when he came out of the bathroom in the back room. He ran his hands over her rear end, and it became a heated kiss. His being Army reserve, and him being called up to go far away to a place called Korea, hadn't deterred the love affair. Being twice her age had appeal for both of them.

Many letters were shuttled back and forth across the Pacific over the next three years. Then, suddenly, the Army Sergeant was standing in the doorway of a bar in Monterey. A nervous Teresa rushed to him, and they embraced, but Danny knew something was up.

She took his hand and dragged him back to the last booth. Her brother Hank stood. He, too, was acting nervously as he glanced at the other man in the booth. It had been many years since he had bent over harvesting asparagus in the Nickapopalos family farm, but the bulbous nose and scar from a thrown knife laying open the young face of the family's only son were still as identifiable as they were when they were kids.

Danny put out his hand and leaned into the table. "Hello, Zeb, it's been a long time."

Nervous, but instantly warm to the old friend, he engaged the hand. His left hand playfully touched at the nasty scar. He still smiled. "Good to see you too, Danny. I think about you every day."

Danny laughed. "But do you keep your hands off another guy's girl?"

Zebulon waved his hand. "Mostly, yes, especially when I'm going after his wallet." He chuckled nervously as he looked over at Hank.

Danny followed Teresa into the other side of the booth as his hand washed the peaked cap from his head. Giving the two Greeks the hard eye, he leaned in knowingly. "So what no good are you two up to?"

The two men acted like young boys caught sneaking a cigarette out behind the barn. Danny drilled them with his looks. Teresa squirmed in the corner.

Danny leaned back and sighed. "Oh, shit. You chicken asses are about to do something really stupid." Leaning in and serious, Danny questioned, "Have you two idiots thought about this job for more than a beer or two?"

"Hey, when did the Army hit town?" The voice was booming and with only a slight accent, but for Danny, it was as good as seeing the man walking up from behind.

Danny looked at the two across from him. "Now I know you chuckleheads are preparing to fuck up to the top degree. You're doing something with Paul."

The soldier turned slightly and looked at the man's boots. You can tell a lot about a man by what he wears on his feet. Paul Giodarno had the esteemed reputation for being the only student who dropped out in the sixth grade and never improved from there. "Hello, Paul. Now, go away, Paul. We're having a big person conversation here."

The burly man laughed as he easily swung a chair around to the end of the booth and sat down on it backward. "Well, mister high and mighty asshole, you had better leave then because we're about to go to work."

Teresa put her hand around Danny's arm. Leaning in, she warned him. "Leave it, Danny. Things have changed."

Danny swung his head and looked hard at her. "Are you sleeping with him?"

He might as well have slapped her. "No! Hell no!" She reared back, offended.

"Then what the hell has changed so much?"

Zeb coughed into his hand. "Money."

Danny looked at the two. "You have jobs. What are you talking about, money?"

Hank poked his finger at the table and rubbed at a set of initials carved there sometime in the last fifty years. "Not really."

"Not really what? A job? I saw the truck out front. One of you is still driving for old Sam. Or is it just a broken-down heap out there?"

Hank looked up. His eyes were too worn out to produce tears. "Times have been tough. The crops aren't what they used to be, and now there are large haulers who can move six times more produce up the valley to San Jose and Frisco in a single truck. They haul with a set of double trailers. Zeb hasn't found a week's worth of work since planting. Only Paul was smart enough to go up to San Jo and get a real job."

Danny swung his head and looked at the slightly younger man with a jaundiced eye. "What kind of work?"

"Sheet metal. I'm installing heating and air conditioning ducts in buildings."

Zeb, wanting to be part of the conversation instead of the tagalong he usually was, offered more. "He also does repairs." And in a breathy hurry, before anyone could stop him, he added, "Like the museum in San Jose. That mummy place..." He stopped, knowing he had just stepped over the boundary.

Danny could feel Teresa next to him turn to stone. As he watched her brother Hank, he could see the tiny bricks of defense slowly crumble and wash away by a sea of resolve. The cat was now out of the bag.

Danny understood just how desperate people had become. None of their families ever got far enough ahead to take a deep breath. Of the three, Danny and Teresa were the winners in jobs held the longest, and for the largest paychecks. But even after twenty years and two wars as a Master Sergeant, he still couldn't walk into the bank across from Fort Ord's front gate and get a loan to buy a new Chevrolet. He looked at Zeb's mouth and could tell the hollow in his cheek was from missing teeth. Probably top and bottom. They were probably removed by Hank and a pair of pliers, the same as his family would do if they had to.

He turned to take in Paul. The man was already balding on top and probably would have a heart attack if he had to put on a rucksack and march for even ten miles. He looked at his hands. They matched the beat-up Red Wing work boots he had noticed before. They were both clean and cared for, just hard used.

Danny's eyes softened as he removed the edge from his

voice. "I'm assuming you're talking about the museum belonging to the Rosicrucian church." The man nodded slowly. "So what's there?"

Paul's eyes started to slide over toward Hank—asking for permission. Danny stopped him. "Don't look to Hank for answers. His answer would be, 'Let's have another beer and think about it some more all night.' What's there?" The hard edge of a sergeant needing instant answers from his men for the last three years of life and death slid through Paul's chest like a cold shiv.

"Gold. Lots of it. A lot of jewelry, too. Big jewels the size of chicken eggs."

Danny took in the information. He now had an objective. He needed the lay of the land, and the attack response and retreat. "What kind of security?"

"None... tonight. The night guards are all church members, and it's a volunteer job. It rotates. But tonight, I know the guy is going to cut out around eight and go with his girl up to San Francisco to get married. He won't be back until around three or four. His replacement comes in about five-thirty."

Danny frowned. "What about alarms?"

"There are four doors. All of them have standard magnet switches backed up with pressure switches in the metal jams. You need a key to turn the alarms off."

"Do you have the key?"

Paul sat up and waved his hand as he scowled with his face at something repugnant. "Pfft, don't need something traceable. I have better." He held up a simple little stick of metal. "This is called a hinge key. It removes the pin from a hinge on the top of most air systems on a building. It's like having a skeleton key to any building in the city."

Danny ignored the false bravado. "Why wouldn't they suspect you of having a key if we go through this air system?"

"Because, for one, the cover is very heavy, and two, it had a lock on it the church put on there. Only they have the key. Whenever we have to go up there, they come and unlock the lock, and the guy takes the lock away until we're done. Then he puts it back on and locks it."

Danny thought about the implication of the believed perception of total security. He smiled wryly. "Except we are going to use their hasp and lock as the hinge instead."

His use of the inclusive word *we* was not lost on any of them. Teresa's hand slipped onto his thigh. Maybe it was the excitement of his joining them, or maybe it was a promise for more to come later tonight.

What Danny liked the most was—it wouldn't be a smash and grab like most robberies. For a novice group of burglars, the hours to do the job were a godsend. Danny also knew it wasn't as safe as running moonshine as Teresa and Hank's family and his family had done for extra money. But it would be the best chance Zeb and Paul would ever get to a shot of getting out of the hellhole of being dirt poor in Salinas.

He looked at his watch. San Jose was a three-hour drive. "I need to get some clothes that don't stand out. I'll meet you three in an hour at the Mail Pouch. I also need to find a car."

Teresa squeezed his thigh. "I'm the driver. The car is Uncle Gino's 1937 Chevy Master Deluxe."

Danny started to protest, but Hank cut him off. "We pulled the eighty-six horse out of her in 1943 when Gino was still driving shine over to the valley. It has a straight-eight, and the steering box is the short truck, so it's quick and responsive. The four-twenty-two is solid as we just replaced the hypoid gears last year. And Terry drives. We need all of us on the door. It weighs over two hundred pounds, and it's big."

Danny chewed on the challenge and the information. It was obvious they had been thinking about this for longer than a couple of long neck beers. He nodded as he turned back toward Paul, one last potential problem. "What if the guard gets cold feet tonight?"

Paul laughed. "He won't. She gave him only half a blow job the other night and told him he gets the rest tonight right after the papers are signed."

They all laughed. Danny even felt Teresa join in. She was little more than half his age, but she made him feel like her twenty-three more than his forty-one. "Let's hope he hasn't taken matters in his own right hand and figures he doesn't need her." As they laughed, he turned to Teresa. "I need clothes, and I can't go home now, or Maddie will be all over my ass like a June bug."

"I've got some at the apartment." She smiled. "They may be a little loose, but they'll do." She rubbed the inside of his thigh to indicate maybe more would be in the offering.

Danny smiled. "The Mail Pouch at five. We can grab some dinner up the valley."

Teresa interjected. "Mail Pouch at five-thirty. I've already packed enough food, so nobody will ever know we left town."

They all nodded and left the bar.

It had been almost nine o'clock before they arrived at the museum. The clouds were gathering thick in the late summer air. The winter cold blowing in from the San Francisco Bay was biting and harsh. Danny knew the night would end in rain. He just worried about the dirt road of the ridge route the moonshine runners called the Snake. The summer had provided a nice smooth surface coming up. Almost no dust had meant Teresa had kept the large car at a constant speed above fifty, a speed that would have had troopers on the highway eyeing them.

The museum was a large box with no windows. Bump-outs spaced along the large walls Danny knew were structural instead of decorative. Only the front entrance provided any kind of decoration to the outside. The building, even for its massive size, almost hid in the neighborhood. The four men stood on the top around the large access door. True to his word, Paul slid the hinge key through the hinges, and they were open. He placed them in his pockets with his latex gloves Teresa had obtained from her woman doctor the week before.

The door was heavy, but Danny doubted it was more than two hundred pounds. They climbed down a short ladder and then crawled through the air duct. The access screen was in the maintenance room. Paul looked carefully in the tool chest and chose a center-punch chisel and a hammer. Motioning, they filed out into a dimly lit museum. Many of the large glass cases contained mummies or miniatures of buildings Egyptians lived in thousands of years before. Danny was starting to doubt Paul's judgment until they entered the inner room.

Even in the dim light, the gold glistened and rippled. The jewels glowed with an inner fire. Everything was as Paul had promised, and more. There were vases and burial plates for a king's chest. Gold and painted helmets, rods, hook things and other items one might hold on a throne. All safe in large glass cases Danny was sure were shatter-resistant.

He turned to confront Paul only to see Hank and Zeb standing and watching a bent over Paul. Danny watched as the man inserted a large center-punch into the loop of the lock. It only fit about a third of the way. He then struck the punch with a sharp rap of the hammer, and they all watched as the body of the lock fell to the floor.

Standing, Paul whispered, "They all do it, even the fancy expensive locks."

Emptying the cases into the four bags only took another five minutes. In twenty minutes, they were back in the Chevrolet sedan and moving south through the city. The rain was picking up, and the wipers were clicking back and forth across the window. Teresa smiled a quick draw of her cheeks, and then she was all business as she moved the heavy car through the streets. Danny marveled how she had a certain knack. If she had driven a route once one way, she could find her way back, or adapt as needed, anytime after.

She also knew how many miles she was from one point to another. It was as if there was a permanent map buried under the dark curls.

DOLLY KNOCKED LIGHTLY on the door as she pushed it open. In her hands were a tray of mugs and a carafe of coffee. "I thought you folks might want to join Hooker and Squirt for some coffee about now." She placed the tray on the table. Looking at the mayor's wife, Dolly pointedly asked, "Coffee, Dani?"

The four mugs filled, Dolly withdrew.

Hooker leaned back into his seat and focused on sipping his coffee. Waiting—the game Manny had taught him so well.

The mayor blinked. "So we had a burglary. Why did I never hear about it? Something like that would have made three-inch type on the Mercury News. Hell, KLIV would have been talking about it for months. Were they ever caught?" He laughed at his un-thought-out statement. "I mean, you know their names and even what kind of car they were driving and everything... surely, they were..." He glanced at his wife, whose grip on his thigh was almost bordering on painful.

Her face was stoic. Her coffee sat on the table untouched. Her eyes lay dead, all life washed away. Fifteen years younger than her husband, the forty-four-year-old woman's usual glow of health was now blanched—except for the remaining red rouge lips. Lacking the usual Greek glow and color, they looked garishly like fresh blood.

Quiet as a whisper, she asked Hooker to continue.

Hooker knew he now had the connection he needed. Turning to the mayor, he continued.

"They weren't caught, sir, because they are dead. They died that night. There is a road running along the ridgeback of the mountain running from south of San Jose almost to Prunedale. For the most part, it is generally straight, wide, and smooth. The county maintains it as a fire break and access road, and the State Forestry maintains it for the same reason. It's also is the fastest and most direct route from San Jose to the Salinas Valley, not patrolled by law enforcement. Which is why the moonshiners knew about and used the road called the Snake?"

Hooker opened the folder and withdrew a few 8x10 photos. He looked over at the Squirt. "John, could you close the blinds and turn on the overhead light so the mayor can see these, please." He waited for the silent man to perform the duty.

With the light, Hooker turned the first photo around and paused. "About halfway down the Snake, I would guess the rain had started to make the hard pack Caliche clay into snotty mud. There is a single nasty turn that even today catches people, and they spin out safely into the open field to the west. But if the driver is good, really good, like moonshine runner good, they will be able to catch the trouble and stay on the road. However, my guess is that on the fateful night, something else happened. I think the driver was really good but oversteered just enough. The entire weight of the three-thousand-pound top-heavy sedan leaned on the right front wheel assembly. The wheel cocked under, and the A-frame gave way—sixteen years of fatigue will do that. If Gino had swapped out the stock front end for one from a Chevy Master Supreme, it wouldn't have folded. The Supreme was a far superior framework for taking the kind of abuse running shine on those back roads."

Hooker pushed the first photo over to the mayor. It was a static photo of the cleaned up bent and broken suspension. "My guess is the car rolled in a nose roll. As it came up, the swing of the car popped the driver's door open, and they were tossed somewhat safely out onto the road. But the other four weren't so lucky. You see, in a nose roll, the next roll is the back end makes contact, and this is when it becomes what we in the towing business call an end-over-end, or becomes a mix-master or regular roll, side-top-side-bottom-side-top-side, and you get the picture.

"The big difference is not how destroyed the car becomes, but what it does to the occupants. In a standard mix-master, people are just thrown for a few feet from side to side with ricochets off the top and seats. At sixty miles an hour, a car like this can take maybe up to six or seven complete rolls on the ground. But with an end-over, the bodies are thrown not only side-to-side but from end-to-end." Hooker looked at the blanched face of the man's wife. "Thankfully, in such a crash, the occupants are killed almost outright. There is no suffering."

The mayor still wasn't catching on, but he was drawn into the story. "But someone surely would have reported a wrecked car... even way out there."

Hooker smiled and pushed over the second photo. "There was a little complication. Well, not so little. More like about eighty feet of complication," Hooker hesitated for only a beat. "What you are looking at is a photo taken from road level, looking down into the raven the car flipped into. It came to rest eighty feet down in that riverbed, and forty feet into the tree line. At the time, it might have just been a brush line. Nobody would have ever seen it lying there unless someone didn't do the same with a Cadillac about two months ago. Lucky for the insurance adjuster, there had been an eyewitness."

"So, if they're all dead..."

Hooker put up his hand. "We'll get there, Frank." Hooker stalled, and then asked, "Is it all right if I call you Frank, Frank?"

The mayor, ever the politician, felt the shift in their dynamics. He nodded instead of committing.

Hooker smiled. He knew the commitment would come later.

"The first problem was identifying the old car, and who it had belonged to. The carmakers mark a car with what is called a Vehicle Identification Number or VIN number. You're familiar with it because you have to copy it down off the dashboard when you do certain things like sell or change your license plates." Hooker watched the man as he nodded, but knew he had no idea what Hooker was talking about because he had people to do those things, or the dealer took care of it for him.

"In this case, the VIN tag had been so rusted through the last twenty years I could pass my fingers through the hole where the tab of metal should be. But in the trunk, still wrapped in the oil-paper from Sacramento, was the front license plate. Some parts had rusted, but the numbers were still good." He pushed the photo over for the two to see. "This is what led us to Salinas and Gino."

Hooker took a sip of his coffee and dove into the last part of the story of connecting lost dots.

The carafe was empty, as were the mugs of the mayor and Hooker. Dani, unmoving still, sat with a still full mug of coffee in front of her like something unbidden, which she was afraid to touch.

Frank's tie had long ago gone askew and pulled. The button was undone, and Hooker could see the mayor's Adam's apple moving as if this were more than just a simple story. Hooker could see he now realized there was more to this story of a crime gone wrong than met the eye.

Frank leaned forward, looking at the dozen or so pictures and the four small stacks of photocopies of documents. "So we have four dead bodies in a car, along with bags of loot, but nobody..."

Hooker cut him off. "The bodies were in the car for maybe a total of an hour. Across the ravine, where the small flash floods over time had washed out a small cave—the driver dragged them and the loot, and buried them."

"But you said these guys were not small men. Are you sure this little Teresa girl could drag them very far?"

Hooker glanced at the still silent Dani. He figured she stood a good five-foot-eight before she put on the low heels. With a life of working hard in the fields of Salinas, Hooker mentally bet she could have held her own against most men her size. His fine sense of noticing small things did not miss the tip of a thin, pale old scar running down her right bicep.

The custom dress looked like any other nice dress, but he was sure the sleeves were extended to cover most of the long scar that was hard to hide when you reach for something in the middle of a large dining table as she had earlier.

Hooker's eyes slid back to her husband. "I didn't say she was little. She was from strong Greek stock. During the wars, even the small children were turned out into the fields to do a good day's labor. I can guarantee you the conditions were not nice, but she was more than able to get the job done."

"So how did you find the cave?"

"I didn't. The Cadillac I had to recover did. All of the windows were basically smashed out. As I dragged it up the cliff, it was upside down. The top scooped up a lot of mud and a skeleton hand and arm. Once I heard about it, I remembered finding something shiny in the mud. I had stuck it in the top pocket of my coveralls, which I hardly ever use unless the recovery is muddy. Once I cleaned it up, I started to look into everything." He pulled a large scarab beetle sculpture out of his pocket and slid it to the middle of the table. He watched Danielle *Please call me Dani* Welton as she stiffened to the state of hard stone.

The silence was palpable in the room. Hooker was sure Dani was no longer breathing, but he could imagine the gears in the mayor's head—the future election, as well as an eye toward Sacramento, and the combined reputations of one of the most respected couples in the Bay Area, who sat on many philanthropic boards. His gears turned, but there wasn't the right fit, and Hooker could almost smell the stench of searing realizations.

Hooker quietly eased the tension. "With this, we have recovered and returned to the museum all of the stolen items—all but the twin to this scarab." The scarab was about three inches long. The solid gold body was tinctured with black tars to enhance the carving. The wings were painted on with a paint made from crushed mother-of-pearl and glass made from lapis lazuli. The blue was as iridescent as Dani's dress and broach.

This time, the mayor stopped breathing. He did not have to look. He knew Dani was wearing the broach he had custom made to hold the antique scarab she had from before they were married. There was also a special pendant built the same way so she could choose which way she wished to show off her prize.

Silently, Dani finally moved. Her hands reached tenderly to the broach and removed it. Turning it face down, she slid the catch—releasing the scarab from its captivity. One last time, her fingers lovingly touched the one item she had that connected her to her brother and her first serious boyfriend. She had never stopped thinking about them or loving them both.

She softly slid the scarab to a place alongside its twin. "So now what, Hooker?"

Hooker could see the steel of her pride, but the quietness of her resolve. She had made herself into the person she could be proud of by doing good things for many people less fortunate.

Hooker reached out and covered the two treasures with his hands. As he slowly slid them back, his right hand lifted the fake the museum had given him for the real scarab he had given them. He placed the beetle on top of the now resurrected file and pushed both toward her. "This city has been doing better than it has in a long time. I think Dolly would agree with me; it not only comes from the hand of the mayor here but also from the good works you bring with your name and hard work. You two have a reputation for dealing with a fair and honest hand. You have turned down the easy but dirty money, and worked hard at doing the right thing."

Hooker paused as he looked into the soul of Dani's eyes. "This is all of the research and evidence we gathered. None of this ever was of interest to any law enforcement department. To them, it was just an accident on a country road. Those involved in the investigation were deputized and sworn in as a special squad who only answers and reports to a single judge up north.

"The Rosicrucian Museum is just happy to have their items back. They never wanted any public attention, and they still don't. But I'm sure they could find a place for a good person on their advisory board." He pointed toward the beetle resting on the file. "I believe the replica should fit in the broach cage, as well as the pendant, which looked so nice with the gown you wore at the cancer benefit last month.

"As for this folder, I don't have any use for it. It served its purpose. I think you would be the best person to know how to dispose of it."

She thought a moment of the significance of the two gestures. Her silent *thank-you* was met with a nod.

Slowly, they all rose stiffly as the clock in the other room clicked past the midnight hour. Turning to the mayor, Hooker stuck out his hand. "Mr. Mayor, I want to thank you for taking this extraordinary amount of time from your busy schedule to hear me out."

The man was taken aback by the grace of the young man in the white t-shirt, jeans, and work boots. "Hooker, it had been a very interesting evening, as well as enlightening. If you ever need to talk, my door is always open for you. And please... it's Frank." They shook with a new understanding.

Squirt rose in the dark corner.

Ever the politician, the mayor turned toward the Squirt with his hand out. "And I think it was John?"

"Yes, sir, but I'm getting used to everyone calling me Squirt."

The mayor frowned and looked back toward Hooker as he still held the Squirt's hand.

Hooker smiled. The final brick was now in play. "Mayor, this is John or the Squirt and my right-hand man on this investigation. This next month, he will be entering the police academy as a combined guest of the San Jose PD, the CHP, and the Sheriff's Office. He's the man who performed the final takedown on the Dime Killer last spring."

The mayor turned back to the Squirt with renewed respect and cinched understanding as to why the young man was sitting in on the conversation. "Well, Squirt, I look forward to having you on our fine police force upon graduation." The man was very sincere.

As they opened the door to leave, Dani stepped over to

Hooker for an almost private conversation. "Did you find any dog tags?"

Hooker swallowed and nodded. "And the watch Maddie had given him when he came home from Europe. She has both now. Danny was buried last week up on Mt. Angel. If you want, I can get you the address, or you can talk to Maddie down at the Main Library. I'm sure she would be happy to have your company and go visit."

"I'd like that." She thought a moment. "It was her at the end of the table tonight..."

Hooker nodded.

"I'll let her know to expect you. I'll be seeing her later, I think. I'm sure they're still working on some trashy Ford that they want to blow up on a race track down near Visalia this summer."

The woman smiled. "Her family never did appreciate Fords."

Dolly stood at the large steel door to usher her guest out. She stuck her hand out. "Frank, I look forward to your next term. There are still a few things to fix around here."

The mayor knew who was the real boss and smiled. "Dolly, I look forward to your vote this next election. Thank you for dinner and for a very interesting evening. But since when is the table no longer all-male?"

It was Dolly's turn to beam. "Get used to it, Frank, the times are changing." She turned to Mrs. Welton. "Dani, it was so nice to meet you finally. I have heard so many nice things about you. Please don't be a stranger."

"Dolly, someone introduced me as the most powerful woman in San Jose. I now know how silly it was, and I'm sure they have never sat at your wonderful table. The pasta was to die for, and I really do want the recipe." She glanced back at where Hooker and Squirt were going over some paperwork with Karen. "And the company was beyond expected. You have a wonderful family here."

Dolly moved in and hugged her, whispering, "Dump the stud next Wednesday and be here about three in the afternoon. We'll cook the sauce together while you write down what we add. We can get to know each other better as family should." She pulled away and could tell she had a cooking date for the next week and any other time she wanted. She smiled warmly. "Wait until you meet the rest of the family."

Ever the guardian, Dolly watched until the large Lincoln pulled safely out onto the street. She kissed her fingers and pressed them to the badge welded to the thick steel door skin as she softly closed the heavy door. The number 701 on the badge glowed dully in the dim light.

She leaned against the door as she watched Hooker explain something on some paperwork to the highly attentive Squirt. It had been an amazing eleven years since the young Hooker had stolen into her heart and created one of the most powerful and caring families along the way.

Her words were only for her, but also silently for him as well. "And that, my boy... is how you get a chip in the game."

CHAPTER TWENTY-SEVEN

K AREN HAD GIVEN them a call on a gold AMC
Pacer with a flat tire. It was a little strange
being about a mile out of Hooker's area, but a
ticket was a ticket on Christmas Eve. It was a commercial
call, so there was no hurry, and the back way took them past
a Thrifty's.

The two young men were laughing as they enjoyed
their matching triple scoops of French vanilla ice cream in
sugar cones. The windows were rolled down, the heater was
blasting toasty bliss, and Hooker didn't even have to feel
down next to his seat to know Box had his one eye closed as
he leaned into the blast of summer-like heat.

As they rolled into the parking lot, the Pacer was pretty
obvious. The older man leaned against the only car in Sarah
Winchester's Mystery House parking lot. The younger man
dressed in a similar uniform and gently rolled himself back
and forth in his chair. Both were smiling.

Hooker groaned with a smile. "Do you see a flat tire anywhere?"

The Squirt snorted. "Dude, we've been had... but I bet my knife could do some fast work on Father Damian's tires."

"I don't think either father would stoop so low or be stupid enough to drive a Pacer."

They rolled alongside but remained in the cab licking the last of the ice cream. Hooker concertedly did not look out and down, but instead kept studying the entrance to the largest attraction left standing in San Jose.

Ice cream finished, Hooker looked over at the Squirt. They both shrugged. *What the heck, it is Christmas.* They slid out the doors.

Hooker's feet hit the pavement. "Well, looky here, we have the Bobbsey Twins. Merry Christmas, boys."

Father Damian laughed as he took in the matching black leather jackets over T-shirts, jeans, and boots. "Before you start calling people twins, you should have a look in the mirror with you two."

The two tow drivers simply smirked and tipped their heads in unison.

Father McBride eased off the car. "Sorry for the ruse, my boy, but it wasn't a real lie. We just thought you would want to say hi to an old friend." He shook Hooker and John's hands. Appraising the younger, he smiled. "Well, Johnathan, you look like you've recovered well enough to take an early seat at the academy."

The Squirt smiled. "Thank you, sir, and Merry Christmas, too. The doc hasn't released me yet, but I suspect I can start the classes at least. The physical part isn't until the second cycle, and I should be up for it all by then."

Hooker shook hands with the seated father. "Did you put in any requests to Santa this year—a new set of wheels... maybe?" He nodded at the Pacer. "And hopefully not."

The two laughed. "I asked the great red-suit for a 318 Hemi for the chair..." Holding out his hands, "But, as you can see... he is still only just a good story." The young priest glanced at the back end of the large tow truck. "But the other big man gave us all a present we couldn't have even imagined asking for."

Hooker and the Squirt turned around to see what the two priests were looking at. The night urchin still bounced his fingers along the working bed of Mae West. The three one finger bounce, followed by the flourish, the double bounce, the hand clamp with a wobble spin of the hand, and then repeated. Each cycle took the exact same three feet of bed to accomplish. The first difference Hooker noticed was Peter looked like a man instead of a cluster of wind-blown detritus. He was still a homeless person living on the street, but nonetheless, a person.

Then the change hit Hooker. Peter was walking toward the four of them. The shy man seemingly afraid of everything, the man who had stayed only in the shadows, and was okay only if Hooker stayed in the cab of Mae West, was now walking in the open, with just a slight hesitation.

"Hello, Peter," Hooker called softly.

"G... goo... hello ho... Hooker." The man turned and took in the Squirt, who nodded softly with a safe smile. Peter froze. Old habits seemed to war with new trials. The twitch was physically perceptible, like a wall switch being thrown. "Yo... yo... you." Peter scrunched his eyes and face closed as he struggled. The other four waited patiently.

The face on the man only relaxed a little, but the eyes were still closed. "You... you saved Hooker." His face opened, and he smiled with open eyes.

"Yes, Peter. My name is John, but I would like to be your friend also, so you can call me Squirt."

Peter gathered his hands to the top of his chest at the sight of the offered hand. The Squirt withdrew the hand, and Peter relaxed some. "Yo... y... can... Candy..."

"Yes, I'm Candy's little brother."

"Ca... ca... Candy... Candy went away." The man frowned.

The Squirt was lost. He looked to Hooker for help.

"Peter, Candy is going to school to be a nurse so she can help people. I know you and Jerry miss her, but maybe she can come visit you on occasions."

The man smiled. "Tha... Hoo... th..." The man relaxed and sagged with a glow. "Nice."

Damian offered the explanation to Peter's transformation. "Peter is now using the rectory's back door. He's trying to make it to dinner with us on a better schedule and has started taking advantage of the temporary facilities we have set up near the alley to provide a safe place for those like Peter to clean up. Clean clothing is the next step, but one push of the wheel at a time." He smiled at Peter. A father couldn't be more proud of a child who brought home a gold sticker.

Father McBride cleared his throat.

Damian came back to matters at hand. "Peter, we will be having a special Christmas dinner later today, so please make sure to be there. I hear some of the good sisters are baking some special rolls... and I know you like a sweet roll."

"O... okay."

Hooker watched the man turn and leave... but true to the nature of the beast, he was almost invisible by the time he was twenty feet past the end of the truck. Hooker shook his head and looked back at the man in a wheelchair—the former Special Forces Ranger.

It was as if Damian could read his mind. "I don't know how he does it. He would have been extremely deadly in Vietnam." His sight moved from where the man had been to Hooker. "Have you ever noticed he doesn't make a sound? The only time you ever hear anything is when he is sort of announcing himself."

"The little rustle of leaves or something..." They nodded as all four looked back into the night.

Father McBride cleared his throat again. "I'm sorry, boys, but we have a place we need to go to before we are needed to get up in the morning."

Hooker chuckled. "I hope you weren't planning to use this car."

Damian cringed. "It just happened to be sitting here. Actually, I think it's been sitting here since last summer."

The Squirt snorted. "Someone got smart and just walked away while they could."

"We just used it because we wanted to surprise you. After all, lads, it is the night of gifts." McBride smiled.

The radio squawked in the cab of the truck. Hooker shook hands quickly as the Squirt hurried around the truck.

"1-4-1." Hooker checked in as he waved and nosed the large truck out onto the street.

Karen's voice came across the tinny speaker without any inflection. "1-4-1, you need to go to the barn at the Romero Hacienda, now."

Hooker's heart stopped. It was well after midnight. Manny and Stella would be asleep... and then he remembered what day it was.

"What's up, Karen?"

"Hooker, it's all I have. Dolly just said you were to go there now. If you plan to argue... then you need to take it up with Dolly."

"Is she there?" Of course, she was there. It was night— Dolly was always there.

"She is... indisposed."

The communication was sharp, curt, and delivered deadpan. Hooker knew the only way he could find out what was going on... was to head for the barn.

"10-4."

Hooker hung the microphone back behind his head. As he leapfrogged the gears utilizing all 1,600 horses under Mae's hood, the asphalt slid past his wheels. Soon, the white dashed lines in the center of Winchester Boulevard smoothed to a static riffle.

Quietly, the Squirt slipped his seatbelt on and pulled it tight. "What do you think?"

Hooker shook his head. He glanced over at the kid. He jammed down through the gears as he got ready for the left turn at Blossom Hill Boulevard. As he pulled the large steering wheel and danced the clutch and gears, he filled the kid in on the importance of Christmas Eve.

"Manny and Stella got married on the dock next to the troopship Manny took to Korea. It was Christmas Eve. Stella's best friend in the world, Claire, came to be her Maid of Honor. After they had watched the ship make the turn in the bay to head out of the Golden Gate, they hitched a ride on a Navy boat over to San Francisco. They danced the night away at the USO. It became their tradition while Manny was over there.

"When Manny came back, he insisted they continue... and the girls have been doing it ever since."

"Without Manny..."

"Without Manny." Hooker twitched his head and glanced over. "Back when I was... well, a kid—Willie and I had made buckets of hot cocoa and chocolate chip cookies. I was out looking for the other drivers who were working on Christmas Eve, and Dolly asked me if I'd take a special call.

"It sucked to work Christmas Eve because it usually means you either were desperate for money or you had nowhere else to go. I just thought the other guys should get a little of what I was getting with Uncle Willie. So there I was—two full thermoses of fresh hot cocoa and a few dozen warm cookies. The girls were dressed to the nines from their high heels up to the ribbons in their hair... and a conked out Caddie on the side at Guadalupe Parkway and the new 280."

The kid rolled his eyes. "Nice part of town..."

"Exactly. I think it was the first time the truck had ever

been close to a hundred. It was a piece of shit Chevy one-ton.

"Anyway, Dolly never let on as to who the ladies were. Manny stayed on the phone the entire time with Dolly constantly mother henning me to death. The girls kept giggling every time Dolly would ask where I was—how were the ladies—how was the tow going—did I have an ETA...? It was annoying, but it kept the ladies amused."

Squirt chuckled. "Along with the chocolate and chocolate..."

"Exactly... But then, they don't understand French vanilla the way we do." Hooker's right hand dropped and found Box's ear. It was warm, and he could feel the deep rumble of Box's contented purr.

"So the Caddie had to go back to the dealer up in Palo Alto, so I had to take it down around the horn and up the 101. By the time we made it back to Hacienda Romero, we had sung every Christmas carol we knew at least a half dozen times, including a few with an open mic for Dolly and Karen. We didn't know Manny was also listening." Hooker looked over at the Squirt and laughed. "After I first moved in... Manny just told me never to sing again."

Downshifting, Hooker took the right and headed down Almaden Expressway. All the lights were blinking red at the intersection. Hooker figured taking the turn at thirty was close enough to stopping. "So that was how I met Manny and Stella."

"So what happened tonight?"

"I don't know. I walked out of the hacienda with some

goofy assed kid this morning, and I've been going ever since." He glanced over. "Have you heard anything?"

The kid looked out of his open window and scratched the scar behind his ear. "Nah."

Hooker turned up what he called *The Hill of Stupid*. The developers had taken a single rural road and turned it into a mass of streets and houses. If the oversized English Tudor-like houses weren't stupid enough, naming the streets with Spanish names—without any knowledge of meaning—was even worse. Hooker turned onto Calle Bonita Verde Avenida, which meant Street Beautiful Green Street... the only thing green was the money people threw away on houses built so fast they didn't work right.

Hooker recalled a bad rainstorm had resulted in him having to tow a car out of a garage at the bottom of the driveway. The runoff that should have stayed on the street was diverted down the driveway and filled the garage to the door handles of the new BMW. The developers fix afterward was to drill drain holes in the wall at the end of the garage so any new water would flood the back yard.

As Hooker pulled Mae up onto her parking pad, he was confused. The hacienda was all but dark like it normally was. Only the gate lamp and the front door lamp were lit. The interior was dark except a glow in the kitchen.

Hooker and the Squirt exchanged concerned frowns as they slid out of the truck and walked down around the driveway. The large driveway would easily hold Mae, but she had her own thick concrete parking pad. As they rounded the house, the parking lot—the size of two football fields—was full to capacity, but the lights in the barn were also dark. Hooker could see the large barn door, large enough to accommodate Mae, or any other commercial truck tractor and trailer, was slid open.

As they crossed the large parking lot, Hooker noted a small Devco milk truck parked with its nose to the basement apartment's windows. When Hooker had last seen the truck, it was white and rust in the back end of Willie's garage. Now it was red and looked brand new. There was a large bow with a large card on the back door—hiding a drop gate... *Merry Christmas, Damian*. Hooker noted the handicapped sticker next to the chaplain symbol painted prominently on the bumper. This must have been Willie's secret project.

As they approached, they could hear two soft female voices starting to sing the sleigh song. Hooker smiled. That night in the truck, nobody could carry a tune in a bucket. They still couldn't, but it was warming to hear Stella and Claire's voices. Hooker looked at the Squirt, and on the nod, they belted out the refrain as they walked through the dark doorway.

A soft glowing object floated in the middle of the dark barn. Glowing arms and bare feet stood below the face...

"Sissy...?"

The black of night shattered into many colors of light as a tall Christmas tree behind his sister, exploded in front of them. The tree appeared to be well over twenty feet tall and towered over the mass of people standing around and in front of the multitude of ornaments and lights.

In the center, walking toward them was Candy and Sissy.

As Hooker and John met them, the crowd was hushed. Candy took Hooker and John's hands as she too turned to face what Hooker had come to know as his family. Sissy snuggled in between Candy and Hooker and put her arm around Hooker's waist—leaning her head into his leather-jacketed chest. "They knew we four had never had Christmas, so they decided to have one that would be special for everyone."

Sissy put her other arm around her new sister's waist as well. It was only a second ahead of Candy's arm finding her.

As the crowd started singing *We Wish You a Merry Christmas*, Hooker leaned close to Sissy. "Have you met Danny yet?"

She softly chuckled. "I want to take him home. But he has a serious problem with my name."

"Claire?"

"Sissy." She hugged Hooker tighter. "I told him it was his problem, so he had to be the one to come up with a name he liked." She looked up and smiled at Hooker. "I gave him until next Christmas."

Hooker leaned over and lightly kissed her forehead. "Merry Christmas, Sissy."

"Merry Christmas, Hooker."

Out of the corner of his eye, Hooker saw Father McBride walk through the large door as he wiped at his eyes. Hooker knew the other priest would take a while longer in the parking lot.

SNEAK PEEK

A SOUTHSIDE HOOKER NOVEL

BOOMTOWN

CHAPTER ONE

Milpitas was a thug town.

The reputation didn't bother Felix. In fact, he liked it. Felix knew he was a thug, and so he fit in—disappeared.

Felix hadn't always been a thug, and he hadn't grown up in Milpitas. He found Milpitas because of its reputation, and he had worked hard to fit into the reputation.

His left hand held a winding of solder as the tip of the small soldering iron in his right hand turned the wire into a tiny bead of liquid silver. The solder melted and flowed around the connected wires to form a solid electrical bond. It became an almost indestructible joining, which only three ounces of custom cooked explosives could, and would tear apart... which was the idea. The formed wires would become so many three-inch pieces of thin metal wire... easily missed in the rubble of what used to be a building.

The cool evening was turned colder by the low mist from the San Francisco Bay. The chilly mist was pushed down the bay by the inflow of sea air squeezed between the Marin County hills to the north and the hills of the city of San Francisco, south of the Golden Gate. This natural squeeze gave the gentle breezes more power as they moved the colder air south over the late winter bay. Milpitas was aligned to receive more than its fair share of the bone-numbing chill, but Felix knew from experience the real cold weather was soon to come. Summer on the San Francisco Bay could rival the cold of many winters elsewhere.

As the light breeze blew into the screened sleeping porch where Felix worked, it drew out a rare smile from the man's face. It reminded him of the shoulder seasons in his childhood home of Colorado. He slid his bare feet into the thick wool slippers his sister had made for him, the sister who still lived on—and clung desperately to—the family ranch. The sister, who still believed, even at forty-eight, her prince would someday come and help her on the ranch, herding the cows and sheep so she could milk the goats.

Felix's toes curled and dug at the home-sheared, washed and carded wool. He humored himself to think his toes could feel the difference in the yarns where her thumbs worked the spin instead of the looser, small fingers in a trailing feed of the large wheel spinning wheel. The small upright would have given her more consistent yarn, but she insisted on using the spinning wheel, which was taller than she stood—because it was the one their grandfather had made for their grandmother when she had to leave hers behind in Boston.

The sweet smell of rosin in the soldering flux curled up from the last soldered connection.

Unplugging the small iron, Felix placed the iron in the holder and gently placed the remaining wad of soldering wire in the cubby next to the iron's cubby.

The last of the forty pieced-together wires were complete. In less than a week, they would just be small pieces of copper once again. Bits and pieces easily lost amongst the debris after an explosion in a store. He pushed them into a long cubby set into the porch's exterior wall.

Felix pulled a square box from its cubby. The box contained tiny vials made of thin glass, the size of a large vitamin pill. He withdrew the first vial and wiggled the small pea-sized drop of mercury inside. He smiled at the memory of coming up with this way to make a progressive explosion without long wires or fuses. The mine he and his father had been sealing up was over a mile long. They had wanted not just to seal the entrance but to collapse the entire tunnel.

The problem was they did not have enough wire to make the multiple runs of wire back to progressive loads of explosives. Felix figured out the small capsule of mercury inside a little plastic pouch to be nailed or stapled to the timbers. Stuck in the bottom of the pouch were two wires hooked to a battery. When the concussion wave from the first explosion hit the tiny pouch, it shattered the glass capsule, and the mercury closed the connection between the wires.

This set off the next explosion, which set off the next—until the entire mine tunnel had been destroyed with less than one hundred feet of wire and a few small batteries.

Felix had soldered the short wires to a small stack of

watch batteries. These would be connected to the blasting caps during the setup. There was just enough energy to set off the tiny blasting cap igniting the larger package of explosives. Felix smiled as he slipped each glass vial into the plastic pouch, sealing it all with a touch of clear fingernail polish, completing the small pressure switches.

This next job would only require sixty of the small compression switches and a few of the larger explosive triggers. The bottles of propane and white gas in the sporting goods store would do the rest of the job for him. The idea was to create many small indistinct explosions, which would become untraceable, instead of one or two large explosions that would leave a traceable starting point at the center of a blast ring. Felix's success came from his explosions going unexplained—unlike arson that would reek of accelerant and have definite start points.

Felix looked at the clock, stood up, and pulled on a brown uniform shirt over his white sleeveless undershirt. He checked the polish on his boots and picked up his keys. Putting the last items in their proper cubbies, he placed the sections of boards back on the wall. He felt as much as heard the click of the small, rare earth magnets drawing the boards into place. The wall looked as it had for the last sixty or eighty years... once painted but now left to chip and weather. He peeked in his now empty coffee mug. He had hoped for one last swallow.

He would pick up a couple of donuts and more coffee on his way to work.

Walking in front of the old dining table pushed to the wall and used as his workbench, he pulled the strings on the two old gooseneck desk lamps. Reaching the door, he turned back for one last check. Everything looked the same. It was a musty, almost bare, seldom-used screened porch just like dozens of other porches rimming the bay.

He turned off the overhead light and gently closed the door. The key clicked in the lock, and then the house joined the early morning silence, muffling the retreat of the crepe-soled boots down the hall toward the front door.

The stork standing on the end of the grass fluffed its feathers about its head and resumed sleeping. Dawn was still hours away. The foghorn on the Golden Gate Bridge started its early morning ritual. The long lonely sound echoed down the bay and blended with the engine of the old panel truck starting and finally crunching its way down the gravel driveway.

ALSO BY BAER CHARLTON

Death in the Valley – Book One
Light to Light – Book Two

BAER CHARLTON

ABOUT THE AUTHOR

BAER CHARLTON

Baer Charlton graduated from UC Irvine with a degree in Social Anthropology, monkeyed around for a while, and then proceeded onward with a life of global travel, multi-disciplinary adventure, and meeting the memorable array of characters he would come to describe in his writing. He has ridden things with gears, engines, and sails, and made things with wood, leather, and metal. He has been stitched back together more times than the average hockey team; his long-suffering wife and an assortment of cats and dogs have nursed him back to health after each surgery.

Baer knows a lot about many things in this world. History flows through his veins and pours out of him at the slightest provocation. Do not ask him what you may think is a simple question unless you have the time to hear a fascinating story.

You can find more about Baer at his website.
www.baercharlton.com

www.ingramcontent.com/pod-product-compliance
Lightning Source LLC
Chambersburg PA
CBHW032119020426
42334CB00016B/1010